NICK

Advance Praise for *Trump and Churchill*

"A must read for any Trump or Churchill fan, and anybody that loves history. A fascinating comparison of two giants from two different centuries with a dedication to saving their respective countries."

—PETE HEGSETH, FOX NEWS

TRUMP AND CHURCHILL

DEFENDERS OF WESTERN CIVILIZATION

NICK ADAMS

Post Hill
PRESS

A POST HILL PRESS BOOK
ISBN: 978-1-64293-469-4
ISBN (eBook): 978-1-64293-470-0

Trump and Churchill:
Defenders of Western Civilization
© 2020 by Nick Adams
All Rights Reserved

Cover art by Matt Butcher

Post Hill Press
New York • Nashville
posthillpress.com

Published in the United States of America

*To my parents, for giving me unending support
and always putting me first. I know I am your legacy, and that
means more to me than you will ever know.
I love you.*

CONTENTS

FOREWORD

Nick Adams has written a useful book that puts the experience of the Trump presidency in a deeply historic and indeed civilizational light.

As a longtime student of Prime Minister Winston Churchill and a supporter of President Trump, I have to confess that until I read Nick's book it had never occurred to me to join the two as historic phenomenon.

Yet the minute I looked at the title, with its *Defenders of Western Civilization* focus, I saw how absolutely appropriate the parallels were.

Nick makes a good case that these were the two premier defenders of Western civilization. In our lifetime you could make a good argument for Prime Minister Margaret Thatcher (herself a passionate devotee of Churchill) and President Ronald Reagan (whose eloquence in defense of freedom and strategy for defeating the Soviet Union were historic).

Churchill of course stands alone as the singular person without whom the twentieth century would have decayed into a terrifyingly murderous domination by totalitarians with Hitler, Mussolini, and Stalin creating a nightmare of death, secret police, and mass murders.

As a number of writers have noted, it was the unique courage of Churchill and his indomitable will to victory that sustained the anti-fascist forces at their low point. Had Churchill been rejected by the king and Halifax installed as prime minister, there is little question Halifax would have sought a truce, which would have left Britain at Germany's tender mercies.

If Churchill is obvious as a champion of Western civilization, the case for President Donald Trump is a little more challenging, but in the end I think it holds up.

Reagan was a great president (I campaigned with him and for him in the 1970s and as a member of Congress worked with him in the 1980s and based the Contract with America in 1994 on Reagan's ideas). He had an enormous impact on the world and was the key person forcing the collapse of the Soviet Union (it is impossible to imagine a reelected President Jimmy Carter leading to the end of the Soviet Union).

However President Reagan did not wage the cultural war with the left, which meant that we defeated communism in Moscow but lost to it on campuses. The continuing drift to the left was barely slowed by the Reagan administration and not affected at all by the two Bush administrations.

President Trump is a much greater defender of Western civilization than his predecessor because he is in a much more difficult situation. In many ways the crisis of the West that Trump confronts is much like Britain after the disastrous withdrawal at Dunkirk.

The very seriousness of the current cultural civil war can be seen in the 92 percent hostile coverage in the major media. The three years of unending and dishonest investigations. The guerrilla war being waged by permanent civil servants especially in the Justice Department and the national security apparatus.

President Trump has been attacked and battered twenty times as much as President Reagan was because he is a mortal threat to the left.

The success of the Trump-McConnell team in getting 161 federal judges approved (as of the date I am writing, still more are in process) is a mortal threat to the most effective strategy the left has had. For two generations the left has developed weird un-American left wing ideas and then used unelected judges to impose them so the power of the government was coercing the American people into change.

Trump's strategic genius (a point Nick Adams makes clear) is in understanding that he wants to effect permanent change toward judges who want to enforce the law. The result has been a principle that all district court judges have to be under fifty years of age. The result is going to be at least a full generation of more constitutionally compliant judges.

These are the kind of changes that drive the left crazy and make Trump their mortal enemy.

Since the left was on the verge of destroying America as it has been and replacing it with a radical America, their frenzy at the defeat of 2016 is even greater.

Nick Adams has done a service for all of us and for future generations by tying together the leadership capabilities and moral commitment of these two great men.

Churchill did save civilization in the twentieth century.

Now it is our job to help President Trump save civilization in the twenty-first century.

—Newt Gingrich

PREFACE

If you could sit on a bench and chat for one hour with anyone, from the past or present, who would it be? It's a good question! A difficult one to answer, no matter who you are.

While there are several choices that come to mind, for me it would be Winston Churchill. But if good fortune somehow allowed me to chat for one hour on a bench with *two* people, it would be Winston Churchill and Donald Trump.

Both men have fascinated me for as long as I can remember. Part of that fascination, I think, owes to my own unique background. I was born and raised in Australia, by a Greek father and a German mother, both of the conservative persuasion.

I attended an all-boys private day and boarding school very much in the British tradition, not at all dissimilar to Harrow School, where Churchill went. Throughout my childhood, I spent extended periods in Europe. After graduating high school, I went to the University of Sydney and got the political bug.

It never left me.

Through every stage of my life—child, teenager, student, and political junkie—I was enamored of everything American: the people, the country, the culture, the founding, the individualism, and the seemingly endless energy and optimism.

In fact, the first time I visited the United States, in 2009, I knew instinctively that I had found home. Over the years, I have often remarked that I was an American trapped inside an Australian body.

For the next seven years, I traveled to America as much as I possibly could, becoming a bestselling author and speaking across the country. On July 29, 2016, I made things official. I immigrated.

Three months later, Donald Trump shocked America, and the world, to become the forty-fifth president of the United States, defeating seventeen Republican candidates and the entrenched Hillary Clinton along the way.

I first heard of Sir Winston Churchill from my father, who made me read his speeches when I was a mere twelve years old. It did not take long for me to conclude that he was the greatest figure of the twentieth century, and for him to become my lifelong political hero.

Just a couple of years later, when I was fourteen, my friend Sanjay gave me a copy of *Trump: The Art of the Deal*, beginning a fervent admiration of Donald Trump that lasts to the present day.

But looking back, while the European background, conservative disposition, Australian setting, and love of America (in the case of Trump) drew me to these men, I see there was something far more binding. It was personality.

I saw a boldness, a self-efficacy, a strength, a desire within them that were all so uncommon, which personally resonated with me. These men showed a refusal to go along to get along. An insistence to color outside the lines. A resistance to established thinking and those who were and are the gatekeepers of it. A proclivity for swimming against the stream.

While the term previously had been reserved for other prominent politicians in the United States, the ultimate maverick in American politics is President Trump. Correspondingly, if you visit the Churchill War Rooms, there is an exhibit titled *Maverick Politician*—although it must be noted that it is far easier to be a maverick in America than in Great Britain, as the former is so invested in individualism and the latter in the collective. British political culture prizes timidity and moderation, making Churchill's individualism all the more astonishing and impressive!

Of course, on the surface, Churchill and Trump are profoundly different.

▶ One was five foot six and loved to drink; the other is a six-foot-three teetotaler.

▶ One napped every afternoon in his pajamas; the other barely sleeps, period.

▶ One began his career by opposing tariffs; the other, by introducing them.

▶ One was a great orator; the other is a great tweeter.

▶ One was a lifelong politician; the other is an entrepreneur.

But neither man made any effort to conceal his true self or conform to expectations. They were unapologetically authentic. Both, brimming with confidence. Both loved their country. Both intensely disliked, even hated. Alpha males. Clear thinkers and plain speakers. Both prepared to stare down their enemies while standing up for their country. Both inspirational men who believed and openly espoused the power of dreaming and persistence.

It has been a habit now for almost twenty years that whenever I visit England, I seek out Churchill locations such as Chartwell and the Cabinet War Rooms. In the U.S., I've even made the trek to Fulton, Missouri, where Churchill delivered his much famed "Iron Curtain" speech—the greatest address by a foreigner on American soil—with President Truman watching.

Similarly, when I find myself in New York; Chicago; Washington, D.C.; or Las Vegas, I always seek out the local Trump Hotel.

The other reasons, far less consequential, that I am such a fan of Churchill are personal.

Churchill loved speaking and writing. He was a man who wished he could have been born an American (his mother actually was). A man who suffered from gout. He was a gift to the English language, wounding with words and propelling a nation forward with his parlance. Churchill went on speaking tours to America. He got involved in politics very early. During World War II, when the Greeks singlehandedly pushed the Italians almost all the way back to Rome despite being massively outnumbered, Churchill said: "It is not Greeks who fight like heroes. It is heroes who fight like Greeks."

I either relate to or aspire to many of these things! (Although not, of course, to suffering from gout.)

I always enjoyed this anecdote regarding Churchill's wife, Clementine. Someone once asked her, "Why did you marry Winston Churchill? He was balding, he was fat, he drank too much, he smoked cigars—you were a beautiful woman; you could have had your choice of many suitors."

"That's true," she said. "I had a lot of young men offer me marriage, and they wanted to read about history. Winston wanted to create it."

That he most certainly did.

And President Donald Trump is doing the same.

I never thought I would see in my lifetime a political figure who was even close to Churchill. I didn't think it was possible. Then along came the political candidacy and leadership of Donald Trump. He was the leader I had been waiting to see.

I supported him from day one. I believed in him. I was on television and across the media predicting his victory and suggesting he might even surpass the successes of former president Reagan, if he was elected. These are two giants from different eras who warrant our admiration and study and warrant comparison.

In writing this book, I have drawn on nearly one hundred sources, including the writings of Trump, the writings of Churchill, biographers' books, contemporary writing, and the speeches of both men. I have used a diverse range of sources, including both conservative and liberal publications, attempting to use original source materials as much as possible. I have kept the source list at the end of this book simple but accessible. I am incredibly grateful for the work of the writers whose research and analysis I have drawn on for this book. Although it is primarily about President Trump and Prime Minister Churchill, this book also is about the American people, the English people, the world, and the society we live in; therefore, it is part historical, part rallying cry, part sociological analysis. It's written for everyone but with Middle America, the Heartland voter, the blue-collar Trump supporter in mind.

I hope you enjoy reading this book as much as I enjoyed writing it.

INTRODUCTION

DEFINING AND DEFENDING WESTERN CIVILIZATION

"Here, in the United States, we are alarmed by new calls to adopt socialism in our country. America was founded on liberty and independence—not government coercion, domination, and control. We are born free, and we will stay free. Tonight, we renew our resolve that America will never be a socialist country."

—PRESIDENT TRUMP, STATE OF THE UNION, 2019[1]

In this book, I'm going to make a bold prediction. President Donald Trump is going to be a greater defender of Western civilization than Prime Minister Winston Churchill. I admire both men. I see both as serving an incredible role in saving Western civilization; Churchill in the twentieth century and Trump in the twenty-first century. In no way do I seek to diminish Churchill's accomplishments. In fact, without Churchill, Trump

---

[1] Donald J. Trump, "President Donald J. Trump's State of the Union Address," whitehouse.gov, February 5, 2019, https://www.whitehouse.gov/briefings-statements/president-donald-j-trumps-state-union-address-2/.

might not be able to do what he is doing. I believe Churchill's leadership against the Nazis and the Soviet Union developed an important foreign policy handbook for dealing with threats to Western civilization, one that Trump has been able to replicate to defend Western civilization from its threats in the twenty-first century.

Churchill understood, even before he became prime minister, that he and the people of England were fighting during World War II for something more than just their own freedom. After the declaration of war on Germany, Churchill ended a speech (which I will return to later in this book) by explaining that they were defending more than just England. He said, "It is a war, viewed in its inherent quality, to establish, on impregnable rocks, the rights of the individual, and it is a war to establish and revive the stature of man."[2]

More than seventy years later, the United States would once again be facing a war, this time a culture war and not as bloody as World War II. However, the war and the anxieties about the fighting (which by and large would not be physical fighting) had been bubbling under the surface for years.

When Donald Trump won the presidential election in 2016, people across the country were shocked, for several reasons. For hardcore liberals, they were so used to hearing other people talk like them and think like them, they had forgotten that people existed who did not share their same points of view. If you are a liberal professor, for example, you may go months on end without having a meaningful conversation with someone

---

[2] Winston S. Churchill, *Churchill: The Power of Words*, ed. Martin Gilbert (Cambridge, MA: Da Capo Press, 2012), 224.

with whom you disagree; you've likely shut off debate in your classroom so that even moderate Republican or just independent-minded students cannot have conversations, and you're certainly not hearing much intellectual diversity at your department meetings, having successfully worked to ensure that none of those pesky conservatives, libertarians, or practicing Christians have been hired in *your* department.

A variety of books have been written on this theme, specifically about Trump (many are postelection "How did this happen?" books) or that predate Trump but in retrospect help explain what happened. Furthermore, these books help us understand the culture and the times that Trump was coming into; if you're reading this book years after its original publication, I hope you appreciate this short summary of what life in America was like culturally and politically in the period that most shaped Donald Trump's presidential victory, between about 2007 and 2016 (although the Bill Clinton and Barack Obama years certainly played a role as well).

For her 2012 book, *Hidden America*, Jeanne Marie Laskas set out to talk to workers that we do not think of everyday because we do not see them: coal miners, trash haulers, the migrant workers who pick our fruits and vegetables. She spent time working with them and learning from them (in the mold of Mike Rowe's show *Dirty Jobs* or Morgan Spurlock's show *30 Days*). Her book reveals how East Coast elites and the intelligentsia in our country often ignore the people who make America run. Laskas, a writer for *GQ*, by far the snobbiest of elitist magazines, should be praised and thanked for acknowledging her own biases and setting out to find out more about America.

For example, one group she spent time with was gun owners. She worked for several weeks at a gun store and even purchased several guns to learn more about why people enjoy shooting guns and to see what it took to acquire guns and a gun license.

Laskas admits this of her friends and their experience with guns:

> I didn't really want to buy an assault rifle [a term that the gun store owner she worked for repeatedly corrected her on], much less a handgun, but I was curious to know what buying a gun felt like, how the purchase worked, what all was involved. This was admittedly foreign turf. Back home, saying Hey, I'm thinking of buying a gun would be a conversation stopper, taken as either a joke or a cry for help. Nobody in my circle back east had guns, nobody wanted them, and if anybody talked about them at all, it was in cartoon terms: guns are bad things owned by bad people who want to do bad things. About the only time the people where I came from even thought about guns was when something terrible happened. A lunatic sprays into a crowd and we have the same conversation we always have: Those damn guns and those damn people who insist on having them.[3]

Laskas's explanation of the way her friends (read: liberals) view guns could be replicated many times over for supporters of Trump and cultural conservatives, including Christians, miners, oil rig workers, pro-lifers, small-business owners, center-right college students. Liberals don't understand people like

---

[3]   Jeanne Marie Laskas, *Hidden America: From Coal Miners to Cowboys, an Extraordinary Exploration of the Unseen People Who Make This Country Work* (New York: Penguin Random House, 2013), 142.

us, because, with the exception of Laskas, oftentimes they don't take the time to get to know us. On the contrary, conservatives and independents, I would argue, often know more about liberals, being surrounded by them in education, pop culture, and media, than liberals know about conservatives.

Yale law professor Amy Chua, who has also written several books about culture and politics, most famously *Battle Hymn of the Tiger Mother*, and who drew scorn in 2018 for defending Brett Kavanaugh, wrote this about the election of Donald Trump and the people who voted for him:

> *Trump's supporters in the country's heartland see liberals as smug, elitist, hypocritical, condescending, and pampered....* Indeed, there is now so little interaction, commonality, and intermarriage between rural/heartland/working-class whites and urban/coastal whites that the difference between them is practically what social scientists would consider an "ethnic" difference.[4]

For conservatives, Republicans, and blue-collar Democrats, as well as everyone else who makes up the Trump coalition, I think it was shocking to realize that there were other people in the country who shared similar views to them. After being told by the mainstream media that people who wanted reasonable limits on immigration, wanted to have their gun rights protected, and were uncomfortable with grown men showering in locker rooms with underage girls were all bigoted, there was a certain feeling of recognition that came from someone like Donald Trump winning the presidency. Traveling the country

---

[4] Amy Chua, *Political Tribes: Group Instinct and the Fate of Nations* (London: Penguin Press, 2018), 163.

speaking to different conservative and Republican groups, I was amazed at how many times students or adults would tell me that college campuses seemed a bit different after Trump won; leftist students felt betrayed, their ideological bubble having been burst (after all, a nineteen-year-old college student had spent high school and college knowing only President Obama). Conservative, libertarian, Republican, and independent students felt like Trump was a rejection or middle finger to the people they were so used to encountering on campuses: the campus feminists, their liberal professors, the environmentalists. Those in the country-club Republican and conservative movement, the Bill Kristols and the Max Boots of the world, had forgotten what it was like to be a fighter on the ground, to be the leader of the College Republicans group, to be the local precinct captain in a blue-collar neighborhood (trying to understand why Christian, pro-gun, union neighbors voted for a party that despised Christians, guns, and manual labor), to be the small-business owner. Insulated from day-to-day fighting with leftism, the Never Trumpers were, to borrow a liberal word, privileged. And so too were liberals.

What liberals forgot is that many people on college campuses come from backgrounds different than theirs. A college student today might not have the same qualms about gay relationships that a college student fifty years ago might have had, but that doesn't mean he adopts every single political position of the campus liberals. That college student may have grown up in a Christian family or grown up working in the family business, so attacks on people of faith and a widespread hatred of business and capitalism are seen as attacks on them and their values (which they truly are). Or, they may be seen as attacks on their parents. A college student with some liberal views and some conservative views is more likely to hear criticism of his conservative beliefs by professors than criticism of his liberal beliefs. A student may hold pro-gun beliefs and also support gay marriage, but when his professor calls all people who oppose gay marriage bigots, he hears that professor calling his parents, his neighbors, faithful Evangelicals or Catholics perhaps, bigots, yet he knows they are not. And when the professor says the National Rifle Association is just like the Ku Klux Klan or, most recently, a terrorist organization such as the Taliban, he sees that his professor does not truly seek debate and discussion. Every time leftists see a poll about how Republicans don't trust colleges, they spend fifteen minutes wondering how that could be and then return to planning their next presentation, such as "Why Pro-Lifers Are Just Like Al-Qaeda," or their gender studies class, Men Can Get Pregnant Too 305.

Not only students but their parents and other adults are seeing this too. In many ways, the rejection of Hillary Clinton and the election of Donald Trump was a sign that people had had enough, and that the silent majority had been awakened. They saw what was going on in their communities, in their schools, and on the television, and said they had had enough. They wanted to see a restoration of Western civilization, even if they didn't articulate it that way. But they knew they supported things like free enterprise, the rule of law, and the ability to have discussions on hot-button issues like transgenderism, immigration, and taxes without being labeled, respectively, a bigot, a xenophobe, or a Wall Street fat cat. They wanted to see their values, the same values Western civilization holds, restored and defended.

Another book that was written decades before Trump's election but explains his appeal is *Street Corner Conservative* by William Gavin, published in 1975. Gavin worked for Richard Nixon, who appealed to the silent majority, a term Nixon is credited with inventing.

Here's what Gavin has to say about blue-collar voters and cultural conservatives: "There is a deep and permanent gulf between urban conservatives and liberal intellectuals and politicians.... The liberal elite have abused and neglected and philosophically attacked the urban conservatives too long for the urban conservative to forget about it."[5]

The urban conservative Gavin talks about is the blue-collar voter, the person who may sometimes vote Democrat but is a street-corner conservative; he is tied into his community, his city. He doesn't like seeing crime left unchecked, beggars allowed to harass women and children, and police officers being called pigs or racists for trying to fix those two problems (especially because the street-corner conservative knows that racial minorities benefit the most from crime reduction and are harmed the most by crime allowed to run rampant). Whether or not street-corner conservatives say it, they support the basis of Western civilization.

Before we continue, let's define the term "Western civilization." It is popular now on many college campuses to say that it means the ideas of old, dead, white men. Or to say that it is a code word for white supremacy. "Western civilization" means no such thing, no more than "Eastern medicine" or "Eastern

---

[5]   William F. Gavin, *Street Corner Conservative* (New Rochelle and New York City: Arlington House Publishers, 1975), 138–139.

philosophy" is a code word for Asian supremacy. Rather, it refers to a set of values and ideas developed in Western society, primarily in Europe and the United States. It has been developed and refined throughout the ages, and furthermore, it has been applied to various populations.

For example, the ideas of Western civilization were known during the 1800s, even if the freedoms associated with it were not always extended to everyone, such as Catholics and slaves. We can judge people by how well they apply their stated values without criticizing the lack of those values in themselves. Whether or not the early colonists truly allowed for religious freedom for all does not affect the value of religious freedom in totality.

What should be agreed upon is that even the people excluded from these benefits of Western civilization in the past support them; they were rightly upset and indignant that they were not granted the benefits of Western civilization, which they cherished.

In fact, critics of the American colonists in the 1800s implicitly agree with the values of Western civilization by criticizing people of that time for not extending those rights to all people. Criticizing people, and rightly so, for not allowing women to have full equality by denying them the right to own property endorses the idea that the right to own property is a positive value. Similarly, arguing that Early Americans did not allow slaves their full rights to be free (by definition of their being slaves) does still endorse the idea that there is a set of values and ideas that makes up what it means to truly be free.

When I talk about Western civilization in this book, here are the ideas and values I'm referring to:

▶ A respect for religious freedom, including the rights of people to worship in the religion they choose or to not worship in a religion at all. It means that the government and society at large respect the rights of Catholics, Muslims, Jews, Hindus, Buddhists, Evangelicals, and so forth to pray publicly, to open schools that teach religious values, to run for office or be appointed judges, or to share their faith in any other voluntary, nonforceful way they choose. Donald Trump has famously stood up for this multiple times throughout his presidency, including against the disgusting anti-Christian attacks by Bernie Sanders against Russ Vought, and against Senator Dianne Feinstein's anti-Catholic rant against judicial nominee and now federal judge Amy Coney Barrett. Feinstein said in reference to Barrett's Catholic faith that the "dogma lived loudly within you," a despicable comment that would rightly be condemned as anti-Semitic or anti-Muslim if said to someone of either faith.

▶ A right to the freedom of speech, including the right to criticize or praise one's government; to write books, pamphlets, or on social media about one's views on any issue, including the right to speak out against the government without fear of reprisal. It's worth nothing here that despite the fake news media's screeching against Trump, he actually is known to be one of the most talkative and open presidents of recent times, and even among all politicians, going back to his old days as a businessman in Queens, New York. Some have even said that Trump is friendlier to the press than President Obama, of "tap the AP's phones" fame.

▶ Democracy.

▶ Support for free enterprise, including a system of limited taxation, property rights, the right to open a business, the right to be free from government corruption and coercion, and a promise that the government will not punish someone for marrying business practices with religious and philosophical views (for example, not punishing Christian bakers for not making cakes for homosexual weddings). This view is central to Western civilization's values, because it reinforces the idea that we have the right to control our own destiny. We choose which religion to worship, we have the opportunity to create our own economic opportunities, and we have the right to the fruits of our labor, in terms of both money and what we buy with it.

▶ Respect for both men and women, including equality in the right to vote, to hold office, and to freely choose one's spouse, and protection against violent crimes like rape and genital mutilation. Although Trump has been erroneously accused of refusing to defend a federal ban on female genital mutilation,[6] he and the Department of Justice are actually in support of the

---

[6]   Bob Cesca, "Shocker: Trump and Barr Refuse to Defend Ban on Genital Mutilation," salon.com, May 14, 2019, https://www.salon.com/2019/05/14/shocker-trump-and-barr-refuse-to-defend-ban-on-female-genital-mutilation/.

law, but after it was struck down by a federal judge, Trump urged that Congress fix the law first in order to apply the law more quickly, avoiding long court battles.[7]

▶ By its nature, a Western civilization–based government and people must also speak out and oppose systems that would strip away these rights, such as racist, eugenicist fascism; anti-religious communism; and the hateful ideology of all other totalitarian ideologies, including fascism, communism, and a caliphate. All these hateful ideologies are a form of collectivism, which is the ideology most opposed to Western civilization, because it seeks to impose on all people a top-down approach that decides who has value and who does not. Communists say capitalists do not have value; fascists say Jews do not have value; caliphates say that non-Muslims do not have value. All these systems inherently violate the ideals of Western civilization.

Throughout their time in office and public life, Trump and Churchill both spoke favorably about these institutions of Western civilization, and thankfully so, because there are not many people courageous or intelligent enough to articulate these values in the way Trump and Churchill did so well. As we will explore in this book, both Trump and Churchill had a

---

[7] U.S. Department of Justice letter from Noel J. Francisco, Solicitor General, to Senator Dianne Feinstein, Committee on the Judiciary, U.S. Senate, April 10, 2019, https://int.nyt.com/data/documenthelper/766-letter-congress-female-mutilation/d448fe5dbad9f5720cd3/optimized/full.pdf.

unique combination of skills and gifts that allowed them to be their century's defender of Western civilization, to defend the values we hold dear.

When I speak of defending Western civilization, I also want to lay out my definitions and the principles I'm referring to so that some left-wing professor or MSNBC commentator can't call me a racist or a white supremacist. (Who am I kidding? The left-wingers and the America haters will call me a racist regardless because I like things like guns and low taxes.)

First, this book should not be interpreted as making the argument that Churchill or Trump came down from Heaven or rode in on a white horse to come save us all. It should not be interpreted to mean that I view either man as a saint. Rather, each man certainly has flaws and issues, as we all do by nature of being human. I do mean that they boldly grasped the moment and used their skills to set us on the right course. This book is about the role that human beings can play in creating a thriving and prosperous society that recognizes the dignity and potential of every human being. But for those who are religious, in no way is this trying to compare Churchill or Trump to a saint or to Jesus or God.

Second, I want to make clear that one of the first victories for each man was that he stemmed the tide; he defended Western civilization first by halting the expansion of anti-Western, anti-freedom ideals, and then by moving the ball back in the other direction. Trump himself is not going to fully restore all respect for free speech, police officers, or the rule of law. But he is first stopping the damage wrought by Obama and then reversing the damage by restoring respect to these institutions and ideals. Similarly, while Churchill helped stop Adolf Hitler

and Joseph Stalin, he himself could not completely stop the ideology that had infected the people in their countries, as some of
that sadly still lives on today. He was able to halt their harm and
make progress toward undoing their damage.

Finally, along the way, Churchill and Trump were helped
by other people. Throughout this book I'll speak of some of
the people who helped them, whether directly or through their
writings and philosophy. Again, neither Churchill nor Trump
is a religious savior or saint. They *are*, however, clearly the
best men for their time and the best at stepping up at defending Western civilization, when many around them were unable
or did not step up to the plate. And as a point I'll repeat several times so it does not get lost, Trump is a greater defender
of Western civilization than Churchill, but only because Trump
came after Churchill and is able to benefit from the work that
Churchill did.

We'll begin by looking at a speech President Trump gave
in July 2017 in Poland, about the role Poland had played in
defending Western civilization, as well as about the importance
of Western civilization. Consider these incredible excerpts (the
full speech is at the end of this book), which will kick off our
discussion of the role Trump is playing in defending Western
civilization.

> ▶ "On behalf of all Americans, let me also thank the
> entire Polish people for the generosity you have shown
> in welcoming our soldiers to your country. These sol-
> diers are not only brave defenders of freedom, but also
> symbols of America's commitment to your security
> and your place in a strong and democratic Europe."

▶ "For two centuries, Poland suffered constant and brutal attacks. But while Poland could be invaded and occupied, and its borders even erased from the map, it could never be erased from history or from your hearts. In those dark days, you have lost your land but you never lost your pride."

▶ "For Americans, Poland has been a symbol of hope since the beginning of our nation. Polish heroes and American patriots fought side by side in our War of Independence and in many wars that followed. Our soldiers still serve together today in Afghanistan and Iraq, combatting the enemies of all civilization."

▶ "Through four decades of communist rule, Poland and the other captive nations of Europe endured a brutal campaign to demolish freedom, your faith, your laws, your history, your identity—indeed the very essence of your culture and your humanity. Yet, through it all, you never lost that spirit. Your oppressors tried to break you, but Poland could not be broken. And when the day came on June 2nd, 1979, and one million Poles gathered around Victory Square for their very first mass with their Polish Pope, that day, every communist in Warsaw must have known that their oppressive system would soon come crashing down. (Applause.) They must have known it at the exact moment during Pope John Paul II's sermon when a million Polish men, women, and children suddenly raised their voices in a single prayer. A million Polish people did not ask for wealth. They did not ask for privilege. Instead,

one million Poles sang three simple words: 'we want
God.' In those words, the Polish people recalled the
promise of a better future. They found new courage to
face down their oppressors, and they found the words
to declare that Poland would be Poland once again.
As I stand here today before this incredible crowd,
this faithful nation, we can still hear those voices that
echo through history. Their message is as true today
as ever. The people of Poland, the people of America,
and the people of Europe still cry out, 'We Want God.'
Together, with Pope John Paul II, the Poles reasserted
their identity as a nation devoted to God. And with
that powerful declaration of who you are, you came to
understand what to do and how to live. You stood in
solidarity against oppression, against a lawless secret
police, against a cruel and wicked system that impoverished your cities and your souls. And you won.
Poland prevailed. Poland will always prevail."

▶   "We are confronted by another oppressive ideology—
one that seeks to export terrorism and extremism all
around the globe. America and Europe have suffered
one terror attack after another. We're going to get it
to stop. During a historic gathering in Saudi Arabia,
I called on the leaders of more than fifty Muslim
nations to join together to drive out this menace which
threatens all of humanity. We must stand united
against these shared enemies to strip them of their territory and their funding, and their networks, and any
form of ideological support that they may have. While

we will always welcome new citizens who share our values and love our people, our borders will always be closed to terrorism and extremism of any kind."

▶ "Our own fight for the West does not begin on the battlefield—it begins with our minds, our wills, and our souls. Today, the ties that unite our civilization are no less vital, and demand no less defense, than that bare shred of land on which the hope of Poland once totally rested. Our freedom, our civilization, and our survival depend on these bonds of history, culture, and memory."

I easily could have just quoted every part of the speech, because the whole speech is incredible, but I didn't want you to think this book is about Poland! But let's reiterate the themes that Trump touched on in his speech. Trump spoke of the power of the rule of law, of the need to confront radical ideology, and the way that religion, in this case Pope John Paul II, has the power to keep people going through tough times. Trump spoke of commerce, and of how free enterprise ties people together, and of how the Polish people fought the twin barbaric ideologies of fascism and communism and succeeded in defeating both. In this speech Trump sent a strong message to Poland: the United States is back, and we will always fight on your side for the values of Western civilization. This message is a stark departure from that of Trump's predecessor, who started off his time as president by embarrassing America and making us look weak by apologizing for things we had no need to apologize for.

We are incredibly lucky that people like Donald Trump have stood up for America and for Western civilization, and have stood against the destructive ideologies of communism, Islamism, open borders, and threatening inclusion (as opposed to assimilation, threatening inclusion is when radical Islamists force people to "include" their barbarism and misogynistic beliefs). In fact, many of Western civilization's ideals go hand in hand; for example, leftists say they support women's rights (an actual Western civilization value), but then they want to arm and fund terrorists and patriarchal regimes like Iran's while empowering sharia law, which treats women as chattel. On the other hand, Donald Trump respects women far more than your average globalist leftist, who believes that we should not judge the harsh views of Islamic countries like Iran.

President Trump, during his time in office, has definitively moved the United States back to respecting the values of Western civilization. In fact, he has moved us back quickly, despite having to contend with making up a huge distance, considering the damage his predecessor wrought on the United States's promotion and valuing of Western civilization; after all, President Obama was spiritually advised by the Reverend Jeremiah Wright, who is decidedly opposed to everything Western civilization stands for, as evidenced by his anti-American and anti-Semitic sermons, displaying a stunning lack of respect for religion.

Former president Obama is a Christian, and I am always careful not to criticize someone's personal religious beliefs. But let me say this: as a president, not as a private citizen, Obama and his cronies led an assault on religious freedom and the beliefs of other Christians. This is the same Obama who tried to use the heavy hand of government to devalue *nuns* who had dedicated their lives to living in poverty and helping those involuntarily in poverty maintain their dignity, by running services such as elderly homes for the poor and those without family to turn to. Obama gave credence to the radical and insidious strain of antireligious zealots in his party who essentially booed God at the 2012 Democratic National Convention, because a group of radicals, hell-bent on creating a secular society that worships infanticide, big government, and the all-knowing bureaucrat, believed that the slightest recognition of religion would lead to a theocracy. Then the Democratic Party wondered why blue-collar voters and people of even limited faith and spiritual life found the party too extreme.

Which is why it was a jolt of energy for voters across the country when President Trump was elected. It didn't matter to them that he was not a particularly religious person; what mattered was that he respected *their religious beliefs*. For conservatives and Christians (as well as faithful Muslims, Jews, Buddhists, and so on), it was not so much that they believed Trump was one of them, but that Trump respected them. He heard them, and he wasn't going to trample on them. He may have been married several times, but he didn't look down on marriage as an institution or compare it to slavery (which Hillary Clinton had said before, leading Pat Buchanan to quip, "Speak for yourself, Hillary"). President Trump may have off-handedly joked about the nomination of his pro-choice sister, Maryanne Trump Barry, a federal judge, to the Supreme Court, but conservatives and independents saw him acknowledge his lack of expertise in that area and rely on his habit of picking the very best, turning to leading judicial philosophy groups such as the Federalist Society and the Heritage Foundation to pick judges for him, and this has been a crowning achievement of President Trump.

Trump has restored respect for the Constitution and the rule of law by placing two originalist Supreme Court justices, Neil Gorsuch and Brett Kavanaugh, on the Supreme Court, and getting confirmed over a hundred well-qualified federal judges who respect the rule of law above politics. In fact, many people voted for Trump precisely because of the courts and because it was clear he was relying on advice from good judicial groups like the Federalist Society.

Two telling cases demonstrate how Gorsuch and Kavanaugh rise above politics in their judicial rulings. In one case[8] as a federal judge, Gorsuch ruled in favor of a convicted felon's right to own a gun, even though normal law-and-order Republicans might oppose this. Gorsuch eloquently retorted to Democratic senator Feinstein that he was sticking up for the little guy, by invoking originalism to explain how the law used to convict the man did not support his conviction for the particular crime of owning a gun while a felon.

Gorsuch said of his judicial philosophy:

> By their example, these judges taught me about the rule of law and the importance of an independent judiciary, how hard our forebearers worked to win these things, how easy they are to lose, and how every generation must either take its turn carrying the baton or watch it fall.
>
> Mr. Chairman, these days we sometimes hear judges cynically described as politicians in robes. Seeking to enforce their

---

[8]   United States v. Games Perez, 695 F.3d 1104 (10th Cir. 2012).

own politics rather than striving to apply the law impartially. But I just don't think that's what a life in the law is about....

When I put on the robe, I am also reminded that under our Constitution, it is for this body, the people's representatives, to make new laws. For the executive to ensure those laws are faithfully enforced. And for neutral and independent judges to apply the law in the people's disputes. If judges were just secret legislators, declaring not what the law is but what they would like it to be, the very idea of a government by the people and for the people would be at risk.[9]

In a case as a federal judge, Kavanaugh ruled in favor of the pro-choice political action committee EMILY's List in its lawsuit against campaign finance laws, even though Kavanaugh is presumed to be pro-life. Unlike liberals, conservatives believe judges should enforce the law as written and not use it as a cudgel against their opponents. Several Democratic U.S. senators believe the courts should rule only their way and never in any way that might ever favor a business. U.S. senator Sheldon Whitehouse of Rhode Island is a good example; he regularly embarrasses the state of Rhode Island and, frankly, the U.S. Senate—nay, the entire U.S. Congress—every time he opens his mouth, wasting taxpayer dollars trying to prove that a drinking game that Judge Kavanaugh played was a secret Satanic occult ritual, as well as going on rambling tirades about the Koch brothers or corporate dark money (oftentimes relying on research or campaign donations from so-called dark money groups, oddly enough!). But what worries wacko leftists and

---

[9] "Here's Judge Gorsuch's Full Opening Statement," NBC News, March 20, 2017, https://www.nbcnews.com/news/us-news/here-s-judge-gorsuch-s-full-opening-statement-n735961.

national disgraces like Sheldon Whitehouse is that judges like Kavanaugh and Gorsuch are respected; that's why the left spent so much time and energy trying to spread outright and despicable lies about an honorable man like Judge Kavanaugh, who supports the rule of law.

In Kavanaugh's opening statement, he reiterated his support for the rule of law:

> *A good judge must be an umpire—a neutral and impartial arbiter who favors no litigant or policy. As Justice Kennedy explained in Texas versus Johnson, one of his greatest opinions, judges do not make decisions to reach a preferred result. Judges make decisions because "the law and the Constitution, as we see them, compel the result." Over the past twelve years, I have ruled sometimes for the prosecution and sometimes for criminal defendants, sometimes for workers and sometimes for businesses, sometimes for environmentalists and sometimes for coal miners. In each case, I have followed the law. I don't decide cases based on personal or policy preferences. I am not a pro-plaintiff or pro-defendant judge. I am not a pro-prosecution or pro-defense judge. I am a pro-law judge.[10]*

And he defended these beliefs even during the most disgusting and vicious attack on a judicial nominee in American history. I won't rehash these arguments too much, but suffice it to say, the leftists' assault on Judge Kavanaugh shows how low they will go to ruin a good man. The next time you see a conservative being attacked by the likes of Kamala Harris (who

---

[10] "Read Supreme Court Nominee Brett Kavanaugh's Full Opening Statement," PBS News Hour, September 4, 2018, https://www.pbs.org/newshour/politics/read-supreme-court-nominee-brett-kavanaughs-full-opening-statement.

did some disgusting and very antifeminist things to rise up politically) or Cory Booker (who lied repeatedly and let the city of Newark, New Jersey, burn) or Elizabeth "Liewatha" Warren, remember that the left took a good man in Judge Kavanaugh and threw the nation's largest and most embarrassing temper tantrum, giving in to the demands of their George Soros pals, all while lecturing Middle America on values and morality.

Furthermore, Trump has stood up for free enterprise and American commerce, while also standing up against cronyism and corporate welfare, beginning the return to the Western civilization value of celebrating the entrepreneurs but not the rent seekers, the grifters, and the corporate welfare beggars.

Of course, we know that presidents and politicians do not create jobs, but they can create the right environment for jobs to thrive in. CNBC finance editor Jeff Cox praised Trump's economic prowess in a 2018 column, writing, "Business confidence is soaring, in part thanks to a softer regulatory environment. Consumer sentiment by one measure is at its highest level in 18 years. Corporate profits, owed in good part to last year's tax cuts, are coming close to setting records."

Cox noted that Trump was successful because he pushed forward with a free enterprise agenda, including cutting taxes and slashing regulations:

> Trump's economic program was very simple: an attack on taxes and regulations with an extra dose of spending on infrastructure and the military that would create a supply shock to a moribund economy. On the tax side, the White House pushed through a massive $1.5 trillion reform plan that sliced the highest-in-the-world corporate tax from 35 percent to 21 percent and lowered rates for millions of taxpayers, though

the cuts for individuals will expire in 2025. On deregulation, Trump ordered that rules be pared back or eliminated across the board.[11]

As I write this, Trump's critics and the mainstream media are trying to trumpet the fear of a recession, knowing that fear of a recession can often cause one. If one happens, it will be difficult to seriously blame it on Trump, who has helped foster the conditions for explosive economic growth and a sharp rise in the U.S. stock market. Trump has been a champion for the Western civilization values of free enterprise and economic prosperity as well as property rights and limited government. Because of his championing, businesses and consumers (who are often one and the same) are feeling confident and ready to invest in America again.

If there's another group that Trump drives wild, it's the race baiters and hustlers, because he *refuses* to play their silly left-wing game.

If Trump is a racist, which he has been accused of many times, he's the worst racist ever, considering that racial minorities have praised him for creating some of the best economic prospects for African Americans and Hispanics.[12] Robert Johnson, the first black billionaire and the founder of BET network, has praised Trump for Trump's incredible economic success

---

[11] Jeff Cox, "Trump Has Set Economic Growth on Fire. Here's How He Did It," CNBC Markets, September 7, 2018, https://www.cnbc.com/2018/09/07/how-trump-has-set-economic-growth-on-fire.html.

[12] Howard Schneider, "Trump's Right, Jobs for Black Americans Abound. Here's Why It May Not Last," Reuters, November 25, 2018, https://www.reuters.com/article/us-world-work-minority-employment-insigh/trump-is-right-jobs-for-black-americans-abound-heres-why-it-may-not-last-idUSKCN1NV0CM.

and for helping empower millions of African Americans. The *Washington Times* reports that Johnson said of Trump:

> *I think the economy is doing absolutely great, and it's particularly reaching into populations that heretofore had very bad problems in terms of jobs, unemployment and the opportunities that come with full employment, so African-American unemployment is at its lowest level.... I give the president a lot of credit for moving the economy in a positive direction that's benefiting a large amount of Americans.... I think the tax cuts clearly helped stimulate the economy. I think business people have a little bit more confidence in the way the economy is going, and I think it's beginning to have some impact globally.*[13]

Many of Trump's critics in the media have unfairly labeled him a racist, just as they regularly do to anyone to the right of Elizabeth Warren. But there's a good rule of thumb to remember: when someone is calling you a racist, it's because no legitimate criticism can stick, so they resort to schoolyard name-calling.

With his economic record, Trump has helped defend Western civilization by promoting true equality, by helping move the country toward better opportunities for all Americans, including Hispanics and African Americans, and especially those in poorer areas who are often ignored by leftist politicians except when campaign season comes around. In this way, Trump has defended Western civilization by helping unify the country around the shared goal of a stronger economy.

---

[13] Jessica Chasmar, "Robert Johnson, BET Founder, Praises Trump's Economy: 'I Give the President a Lot of Credit,'" *Washington Times*, July 9, 2019, https://www.washingtontimes.com/news/2019/jul/9/robert-johnson-bet-founder-praises-trumps-economy-/.

It harks back to a brilliant speech Churchill gave in July 1940, as England was preparing for an impending German invasion. Churchill spoke similarly about uniting the country—all people of all backgrounds. He said:

> I stand at the head of a Government representing all parties in the State—all creeds, all classes, every recognisable section of opinion. We are ranged beneath the Crown of our ancient monarchy. We are supported by a free Parliament and a free Press; but there is one bond which unites us all and sustains us in the public regard—namely...that we are prepared to proceed to all extremities, to endure them and to enforce them; that is our bond of union in His Majesty's Government to-night.... But all depends now upon the whole life-strength of the British race in every part of the world and of all our associated peoples and of all our well-wishers in every land, doing their utmost night and day; giving all, daring all, enduring all—to the utmost—to the end.

In other words, everyone must unite around this common cause; all people in the country are equal, and all are expected to fight together to save their country, and by default, Western civilization from ruin.[14] These remarks are similar to what Trump has said in unifying messages (which of course the fake news media try to manipulate or ignore, because such remarks make Trump look good).

We can also look at what Trump has said to show how he defends Western civilization. Consider these Trump quotes, remembering that each one is an authentic statement, laying out Trump's true beliefs and what lies in the depths of his heart.

---

[14] *Churchill: The Power of Words*, 261.

These are the words of a man who loves his country and thrives for liberty and prosperity for all.

- ▶ "America is a nation of believers, and together we are strengthened by the power of prayer."[15]
- ▶ "Anyone who endorses violence, hatred, or oppression is not welcome in our country and never will be."
- ▶ "As your president, I will do everything in my power to protect our LGBT citizens from the violence and oppression of a hateful foreign ideology."[16]

Let's review briefly what Trump is saying here. First, he supports the rights of all people to hold their religious beliefs, or no religious beliefs at all. Second, he strongly condemns violence, hatred, and oppression, and abhors racist ideology. Finally, he melds his support for defeating radical Islam with his conviction that all people, including LGBT citizens, must be protected from the barbarism of radical Islam and hatred of homosexuals. It is, after all, his administration that has made it a priority to end the execution of homosexuals.[17]

NBC News reported in February 2019:

---

[15] "President Donald J. Trump Stands Up for Religious Freedom in the United States," whitehouse.gov, May 3, 2018, https://www.whitehouse.gov/briefings-statements/president-donald-j-trump-stands-religious-freedom-united-states/.

[16] "Full Text: Donald Trump 2016 RNC Draft Speech Transcript," Politico, July 21, 2016, https://www.politico.com/story/2016/07/full-transcript-donald-trump-nomination-acceptance-speech-at-rnc-225974.

[17] Josh Lederman, "Trump Administration Launches Global Effort to End Criminalization of Homosexuality," NBC News, February 19, 2019, https://www.nbcnews.com/politics/national-security/trump-administration-launches-global-effort-end-criminalization-homosexuality-n973081.

The Trump administration is launching a global campaign to end the criminalization of homosexuality in dozens of nations where it's still illegal to be gay, U.S. officials tell NBC News, a bid aimed in part at denouncing Iran over its human rights record. U.S. Ambassador to Germany Richard Grenell, the highest-profile openly gay person in the Trump administration, is leading the effort, which kicks off Tuesday evening in Berlin. The U.S. embassy is flying in LGBT activists from across Europe for a strategy dinner to plan to push for decriminalization in places that still outlaw homosexuality—mostly concentrated in the Middle East, Africa and the Caribbean.... That list includes the United Arab Emirates, Pakistan and Afghanistan—all U.S. allies—although those countries aren't known to have implemented the death penalty for same-sex acts. In Egypt, whose leader Trump has effusively praised, homosexual relations aren't technically illegal but other morality laws are used aggressively to target LGBT people. New U.S. pressure on those countries to change their laws comes as the Trump administration is working to use nascent ties between Arab nations and Israel to form a powerful axis against Iran, a strategy that dovetails with the administration's planned rollout of an ambitious plan for Israeli-Palestinian peace.[18]

Unlike Obama, a weak president, who thought protecting LGBT rights meant forcing Christian bakers to bake cakes or forcing seven-year-old girls to shower with fifty-year-old men, Trump understands that all of us can be united against the horrific execution of people who are gay, while still disagreeing about issues such as gay marriage and transgender

---

[18]   Lederman, "End Criminalization of Homosexuality."

bathrooms. President Trump, unlike Obama, is actually leading from the front on this issue, once again finding a way to unite the American people around the core principle of being free from government force in one's life. He has found a way to unite Americans of all religious and cultural beliefs around objective moral truths, such as it is wrong to kill someone for being gay, while not taking on a more divisive issue, such as gay marriage itself or transgender bathrooms. It's an incredibly good move by Trump to focus more on what unites the country than on what we argue over.

Throughout his life, Churchill expressed similar ideas about unifying ideas and the importance of uniting around common principles. Consider these Churchill quotes:

- ▶ "Socialism is, in its essence, an attack not only upon the British enterprise, but upon the right of the ordinary man or woman to breathe freely without having a harsh, clumsy, tyrannical hand clapped across their mouths and nostrils.... No Socialist Government conducting the entire life and industry of the country could afford to allow free, sharp, or violently-worded expressions of public discontent.... And where would the ordinary simple folk—the common people...where would they be, once this mighty organism had got them in its grip?"[19]

- ▶ "The courage of a soldier advancing in a forlorn hope is not greater, and his ordeal is far less trying, than that of the man—or woman—who, sometimes for

---

[19] *Churchill: The Power of Words*, 360.

years, dwells in the midst of the enemy with his life hanging upon every chance word or action...the services which can be rendered to King and Country may sometimes far exceed in importance the results of the most splendid acts of devotion in the field."[20]

▶ "The search for peace is not the special preserve of any one political party. We are all agreed on the end. It is on how we can best secure peace that we differ."[21]

Now let's review what Churchill is saying in these quotes. Socialism is not just an economic theory that might hurt a few people; it is tyranny disguised as charity. Socialism is tyranny against the human spirit and a violation of the Western civilization value of liberty. Peace must sometimes come with brute force, but it is important to fight to protect our liberties.

This book is full of stories about and quotes from Churchill, but I could easily share hundreds more quotes by both Trump and Churchill to reinforce the point about the importance of Western civilization to both men. They both recognized the importance of free enterprise, the rule of law, limited government, religious freedom, and the freedom of speech, as will be demonstrated throughout this book.

Notice that in these ideals, I am not trying to lay out a specific policy or precise limits on each ideal. This is not a policy book, and there are plenty of people who know more about policy than I do. I make no argument here about whether Western civilization means having a 23 percent top income tax rate or a 27 percent top income tax rate. I do not argue here about

---

[20] *Churchill: The Power of Words*, 145.
[21] *Churchill: The Power of Words.* 426.

whether free speech extends to violent threats or the malicious spreading of falsehoods. Rather, we should view Western civilization as a broad set of ideals, within which people can make trade-offs. (Some may favor a corporate tax rate but no income tax rate; some may justify specific tariffs to protect local industries. In any case, Western civilization still broadly respects free enterprise and support, not the demonization of business.)

This is also not a book about polling data. Values that are true and right do not change when 50 or 60 percent of people disagree with them. The values and ideas discussed in this book will remain true next year, in ten years, and in fifty years. Any references to the views of millennials would be dated in six months when the next set of polling is released. Also, in my view, morality is not a popularity contest. When the majority of America believed slavery was justified, slavery was still immoral. Likewise, even if 99 percent of people said it was okay to lie or to steal, lying or stealing would still be wrong. I am making my arguments based on the principles of Western civilization and how President Trump and Prime Minister Churchill worked to defend those principles and ideals, and how they both did it incredibly well, the best of anyone in their generation.

Now let's get into what this book is really about and how you can use it, as well as what I hope you can take away from it.

As a legal immigrant, I did immigration the right way and followed the proper legal process for people. Like every 2020 presidential candidate who seems not to know the difference, I have great respect for Western civilization and the United States of America. It is this great country of the United States that I fought so hard to join. Had I been alive during the time of Churchill, perhaps I would be fighting to become a citizen of England (not today though, of course!).

President Donald J. Trump will end up in the history books as a greater defender of Western civilization than even Prime Minister Winston Churchill, a man who deserves enormous credit for defeating Nazi Germany and protecting Great Britain, and Europe at large, from being perpetually ruled by fascists. There are many similarities and differences between the two men, and President Trump benefits from the work done by Churchill, much as Churchill would have benefitted from the work done by President Trump if he had come after Trump. But in this book, as mentioned previously, I will argue that President Trump will be a greater defender of Western civilization. In fact, while Churchill may have had his disputes with other European leaders and President Roosevelt, those people were more or less on his side. But Trump is largely going alone at the goal of saving Western civilization, with some help from our allies. Many foreign leaders, however—such as the weak and effeminate Justin Trudeau of Canada—want to be seen as anti-Trump or are wont to be labeled white supremacists or ethnonationalist for working with Trump. Being against someone is not enough; someone must lay out clear policy goals and a vision for how he will be different. This is one reason Trump did better than Mitt Romney; Romney was seen as being "not Obama," and while some people who were "not Hillary" definitely voted for Trump, he also made clear the specific ideas he stands for. He didn't need a five-hundred-page white paper on immigration that was created specifically to make it unclear where he stood. He had clear principles on immigration: deport violent criminals first, build a wall on the southern border, and reopen the debate about what to do with millions of illegal immigrants.

In some ways, President Trump had to use extravagant language to force a discussion on the issue. For example, by calling out the criminal nature of some illegal immigrants, who were giving legal immigrants and otherwise noncriminal illegal immigrants a bad name, he forced the media to begin a discussion that they did not want to have; namely, what our actual plan to fix the problems of overstayed visas and unchecked migration is. By forcing the media to cover his comments, he was able to reach people who shared his view; in general, immigration and immigrants are a good thing, but that doesn't mean we can't have, as Michael Savage would say, our own border, language, and culture.

I never thought that a leader would come along who could outdo Churchill. And nothing in this book should be taken as denigrating a great man; in fact, as mentioned previously, it is impossible that Trump could accomplish what he has accomplished without the tremendous work Churchill did, or without what he learned from Churchill. It is a simple fact of linear time that whoever comes last has a chance to outdo a preceding person, just as Churchill was a better leader than any prime minister or Western leader before him.

And it has often been reported that President Trump's hero is Prime Minister Churchill. After all, one of the first acts that Trump took as president was to bring the bust of Winston Churchill back into the Oval Office.[22] In July 2018, Britain made

---

[22] Theodore Schleifer and Kevin Liptak, "Trump Brings Churchill Bust Back to Oval Office," CNN, January 20, 2017, https://www.cnn.com/2017/01/20/politics/trump-churchill-oval-office/index.html.

sure to play to Trump's interest in and adoration of Churchill, including letting Trump sit in Churchill's chair at Chequers.[23] And in June 2019, the queen of England gave Trump a book by Churchill about World War II.[24] This infuriated leftists and drove them completely bonkers, because they so wanted the queen to hate Donald Trump like they hate Donald Trump.

Others have drawn similar comparisons between Trump and Churchill, and understandably so; both are great men known for serving their country admirably. There will be critics of this book. People will say that neither man was that great, that each had great people behind him, or that both were racists, white supremacists, and/or nationalists. Yet, great minds in Middle America, not just in the intelligentsia, can see that a strong leader who can take decisive action, even if that person has flaws, is often what it takes. There is a trend today in modern academia and in Hollywood to go back and look at everything someone who was great did and try to find a reason to hate that person. For liberals, this makes sense. They hate success. They hate those who make good decisions and take responsibility. It only makes sense that they would take a billionaire like Trump, whom they liked when he was in the New York social scene, and go back and revise history to fit their notions. As I write this, George Washington and Thomas Jefferson are being portrayed as virulent racists, because what they did in the late 1700s and

---

[23] Meg Wagner, Brian Ries, James Masters, and Veronica Rocha, "President Trump in the UK," CNN, July 13, 2018, https://www.cnn.com/politics/live-news/trump-uk-visit-2018/h_8310ae4d4fd15657086af9710834186d.

[24] "Queen Gifts Trump a Book on World War Two," Reuters, June 4, 2019, https://www.reuters.com/article/us-usa-trump-britain-gifts/queen-gifts-trump-a-churchill-book-on-world-war-two-idUSKCN1T516X.

early 1800s wasn't perfectly aligned with our more advanced moral system today. Slavery is awful, but Jefferson and Washington were still more pro-freedom than many in their time.

Writing for the website Townhall, William Marshall notes:

Our politics are roiled by tensions between a large (largely young), ignorant population of idealists taken in with the concept of socialism/communism and an older, wiser populace who recognize the greatness of the contributions of our country. We face external enemies today as ruthless as those faced by England in the '30s. Our alliances are complex and our national fiscal situation is deeply concerning, just as the UK's was. The similarities between Britain of that era and America of today, to my mind, are almost eerie. And the similarities between Donald Trump and Winston Churchill bear description....

While Donald Trump may not have possessed a deep grounding in conservative philosophy before his ascent to the presidency, he's demonstrated that he possessed something far more important: a love for America as its Founders envisioned it.

In the same way, Winston Churchill understood how the British Empire lifted so much of the world out of darkness and into a better, more civilized place—with education and healthcare provided for the poor, markets for the industrious to sell their wares and thereby raise their station in life, and administrative and legal structures to provide due process and equal protection under the law. I, for one, feel reassured that we have the equivalent of the British Bulldog sitting in the White House. Let us hope that President Trump has as

*successful a tenure as head of state as did Winston. He seems
well on his way.*"[25]

Marshall is a former intelligence analyst who understands
the threats that have faced this country—and he makes the
strong argument that Trump and Churchill share many similarities. A fighting spirit. An appreciation for markets. And a will
to make life better for the people he served. Marshall truly hits
the nail on the head. Let's break down what else he is saying.
Trump is a bulldog. A bulldog is not the most loving or cuddly
of dogs (though some certainly are), but a bulldog is a practical
animal. It's a bit rough around the edges. It might come off as
crude, but when a robber comes, people would want a vicious
bulldog on their side. Similarly, Churchill and Trump had flaws;
they weren't the politician-in-a-box, clean-as-a-whistle type
like Mitt Romney, but they were right for their time, and their
bulldoggishness made them the leaders they turned out to be.

Consider what else Marshall says: "While Trump may not
have possessed a deep grounding in conservative philosophy
before his ascent to the presidency, he's demonstrated that he
possessed something far more important: a love for America
as its Founders envisioned it." Many conservatives were wary
about a thrice-married New York billionaire who made money
in casinos representing their party. Additionally, he didn't
seem to be a *Wall Street Journal* or *National Review* reader. For
Heaven's sakes, he read the *New York Times*! But he also was
close to the grass roots of America: Republicans, Democrats,

---

[25] William Marshall, "Donald Trump: America's Winston Churchill?," Townhall, March 28, 2019, https://townhall.com/columnists/williammarshall/
2019/03/28/donald-trump-americas-winston-churchill-n2543898.

and Independents, who turned to the likes of Rush Limbaugh and Fox News. They were the ones who fought for conservatism in their communities, not just at Chamber of Commerce and American Enterprise Institute luncheons. They were, to quote Pat Buchanan, "conservatives of the heart." Trump loves his country. He recognizes, as he noted in an early Republican debate, that to be a conservative means to have the desire to conserve. Free markets and free trade are preferable to communism and central planning, but they are not perfect. They are better because they are better at conserving wealth. But when they go awry, a good conservative can adjust, calibrate, but still stay true to the general pro-entrepreneurship and pro-commerce posture. Samson, of the Bible, wasn't perfect either, but he was right for what he was called to do.

Frank Meyer, writing about the importance of values and Western civilization, said:

> ...[T]he great renewers have been those were able to recover true principle out of the wreck of their heritage. They were guided by reason—reason mediated, it is true, by prudence, but in the first instance, reason. Like Socrates, Plato, Aristotle, confronting the chaos in the body politic and in the minds of men created by the overweening pride of the Athenian demos.... We cannot simply revere; we cannot uncritically follow tradition, for the tradition presented to us is rapidly becoming—thanks to the prevailing intellectual climate, thanks to the schools, thanks to the outpourings of all the agencies that mold opinion and belief—the tradition of a

positivism scornful of truth and virtue, the tradition of the collective, the tradition of the untrammeled state.[26]

Meyer reflected well many years ago in this essay the ideas articulated by people like Pat Buchanan and Donald Trump: that there are values and institutions we want, but conservatism should not mean just worshipping things; there is at the heart of defending and renewing a civilization the idea that people come first, and that a healthy society is necessary, even if that means deviating from a party or ideological orthodoxy (for example, on the issue of trade).

In many ways, this is one way Churchill and Trump are very similar. Others too have drawn similar comparisons between these two great leaders. Former Arkansas governor Mike Huckabee tweeted, "Churchill was hated by his own party, opposition party, and press. Feared by King as reckless, and despised for his bluntness. But unlike Neville Chamberlain, he didn't retreat. We had a Chamberlain for 8 yrs; in @realDonaldTrump we have a Churchill."

For this, he drew criticism, which actually proves his point. The main critics were leftist hacks, Establishment consultants, and those who already hated Mike Huckabee and his down-to-earth conservatism and populism; in other words, the same people who hated Trump. Huckabee could have said that Donald Trump was similar to Donald Trump, and the blowhards in the fake news media would have found a way to criticize him for this statement.

---

[26] Frank S. Meyer, "Freedom, Tradition, and Conservatism," *What Is Conservatism?* (New York: Holt, Rinehart and Wilson, 1964), 16.

A little background on both Churchill and Trump, for those who may not be familiar with both. This book is definitely not a biography of both men; there are volumes written about, and by, Churchill. Trump himself is a prolific writer and one of the best. Additionally, more and more about the Trump legacy will be written after Trump completes his time in office. But here are a few facts, first about Churchill.

▶ He entered Sandhurst in 1893 on his second try, and entered as commissioned cavalry in 1894. At only twenty-two years old, he published his first book.

▶ In 1899, he lost his first race for Parliament, was captured in the Boer War, and escaped.

▶ From 1905 to 1921, he moved in and out of various positions in the government, including home secretary, lieutenant colonel, and secretary for air and war.

▶ Between 1922 and 1924, he lost three elections.

▶ In 1932, at the age of fifty-eight, he entered "the political wilderness."[27]

▶ In 1933, as chancellor, he was confronted with Hitler and Nazi Germany.

▶ He was one of the few Western leaders to accurately warn about the threat of the Soviets.

▶ After losing a race for prime minister, he returned to Parliament.

---

[27] William Manchester, *The Last Lion: William Spencer Churchill—Visions of Glory, 1874–1932* (Boston: Little, Brown, 1983).

Now let's look at some of the successes of Donald Trump so far, both as a politician and in his longer life as a private citizen and entrepreneur.

► In 1968, he graduated from the prestigious Wharton School of Business, at the University of Pennsylvania. It's here where he likely learned many of the key business skills he later used to become a successful billionaire entrepreneur.

► In July 1982, he completed the famous Trump Tower in New York.

► In 1987, his wildly successful book *The Art of the Deal* was published.

► In 1991, he declared bankruptcy but later emerged victorious as a billionaire.

► At various times even before becoming president, he played an important role in shaping political debates in our country, including warning of the threats of China, speaking out sharply against President Obama's policies, and regularly appearing on shows like *Fox & Friends*, educating millions of viewers on his views and building a loyal following.

► In 2016, he shocked the Republican Party Establishment and most of America by winning the GOP primary contest and beating Secretary Hillary Clinton in the political upset of our lifetime.[28]

---

[28] Hannah K. Gold, "Donald Trump's Life and Career," *Rolling Stone*, September 9, 2015, https://www.rollingstone.com/politics/politics-news/donald-trumps-life-and-career-a-timeline-50459/.

As president, Trump has been incredibly successful, so in the interest of space, I'll list just a few of his big accomplishments.

- ▶ He pushed through the confirmation of two originalist Supreme Court justices, Neil Gorsuch and Brett Kavanaugh. He saw one of the dirtiest and most unethical efforts against Kavanaugh play out and still managed to get Kavanaugh confirmed. Additionally, he got a record number of federal judges confirmed at record-breaking speeds.

- ▶ He got passed and then signed massive corporate and individual income tax cuts.

- ▶ The U.S. stock market soared to record levels, and there have been record levels of consumer and business confidence as I write this, thanks to tax cuts, massive deregulation, and the general feeling that Trump supports small businesses and the American dream.

- ▶ He decimated the radical terrorist group ISIS.

- ▶ The country witnessed the complete embarrassment of the Democratic Party, as the fake-news Russia-collusion investigation fell apart and formerly respected FBI director Robert Mueller imploded during the hearing. Similarly, James Comey has left behind a tainted and disgraced legacy that cannot be repaired by his running for office. (What would his platform be: "I was fired by the president, and I hid behind curtains when I was in the Oval Office"?)

In this book, I take a unique look at the developing legacy of Donald Trump and set it against the legacy of Winston Churchill, a man who, we often forget, was also despised by the elites and the resistance of his day but whose decisions and philosophy were, by and large, proven correct. As Churchill saved Western civilization in the twentieth century, so too is Donald Trump saving not only Western civilization but the entire world at large in the twenty-first century, through his decisiveness, his ability to take in information and make quick decisions, and his incredible foresight and courage. Both men took over from weak predecessors, both men at different times had to upend traditional "wisdom." Currently there is a difference that I feel confident will dissipate as time passes: Churchill is now recognized for his ability as a leader, while liberal pundits, coastal elites, and the intelligentsia of the Beltway's think tank crowd in both the Republican Party and the Democratic Party still, after his nearly three years in office, look down on the great work that President Trump has done to save our country, Western civilization, and the world at large.

Trump's role as a leader should come as no surprise. In his book *Trump: How to Get Rich*, he explains how he views his role as the CEO of The Trump Organization: "More and more, I see that running a business is like being a general. Calling the shots carries a great deal of responsibility, not only for yourself, but for your troops. Your employees' lives, to a large extent, are dependent on you and your decisions. Bad strategy can end up affecting a lot of people. This is where being a leader takes on a new dimension. Every decision you make is an important one, whether there are twenty thousand people working for you or just one."[29]

Foreign policy giant and Establishment member Henry Kissinger, former secretary of state, even offers praise for Trump, saying in 2018, "I think Trump may be one of those figures in history who appears from time to time to mark the end of an era and to force it to give up its old pretense."[30] Kissinger of course is one of those people whom society is now going back and hating on because of decisions he made that, in light of the current situation, seem poor or questionable. But that is even a better reason to trust what he is saying about Trump; he understands that the liberal peaceniks always forget how bad things were, bask in the great world that conservatives create, and then go back to find a way to undermine the success of a conservative. Liberals—remember this while reading this book—do not like success. That's why they see places like Venezuela and Somalia and try to import the "values" of those countries into the United States. For Heaven's sakes, as I write this book, the daughter of a Somalian refugee is bashing the United States, forgetting the horrors that the United States saved her from. See what I mean? Thanks to Trump, we are so successful that people are grasping for things to complain about instead of being thankful for the great country in which we live.

Writing in *The Last Lion: Winston Spencer Churchill— Visions of Glory*, Churchill scholar William Manchester writes, "England's new leader, were he to prevail, would have to stand for everything England's decent, civilized establishment had

---

[29] Donald J. Trump, with Meredith McIver, *Trump: How to Get Rich* (New York: Random House, 2004), 3.

[30] Victor Davis Hanson, *The Case for Trump* (New York: Basic Books, 2019), 2.

rejected." In other words, the leader who would restore English greatness had to be a bit out there—a bit eccentric, a bit outside of the mainstream, much like the way a Queens, New York, billionaire oddly was the one who has best connected with working-class coal miners and construction workers in rural Pennsylvania or Michigan or Wisconsin. Manchester said the new leader of England would have to "create a sublime mood and thus give men heroic visions of what they were and might become."[31] He would have to inspire men and women that the country could be made great again! Victor Davis Hanson, in *The Case for Trump*, writes similarly of Trump, "It is unlikely that *any* other politician could have followed the winning Trump formula…." In other words, Trump the person with all his flaws and eccentricities, is the only one suited for the job and for the time.[32]

But Churchill was not always loved by his people during his time. Even now, people are retroactively looking at Churchill and trying to call him a racist, an imperialist, or a nationalist. A book comparing Trump to Churchill might cause people like that to say, "Exactly! I hate them both!" Well, bully for them.

Both Churchill and Trump have a reputation for being hard workers, passionate, and energetic, and for taking on many projects at once in a zealous fashion. *Winston Churchill: A Life from Beginning to End* says that Churchill had "a manic energy and passion that drove him to work tirelessly, staying up days on end working to pass proposals and legislation," and that he

---

[31] *The Last Lion—Visions of Glory*, 4.
[32] *The Case for Trump*, 103.

"was both a vigorous speaker and writer.... Churchill often had so many projects and efforts unfolding all at the same time."[33]

Likewise, we know that President Trump routinely works long days, as evidenced by his late-night and early-morning tweets and the description in *Trump: How to Get Rich* of his typical workday as consisting of numerous meetings, phone calls, and working after dinner for twelve to fifteen hours.[34] Of course, his critics in the Establishment media and the consultant class view this as a flaw, preferring the sleepiness and low energy of a president and secretary of state who could not be bothered from their slumber to save brave U.S. foreign officers who were in the midst of a fire that the secretary of state and president themselves created. (For the future generations reading this, Hillary Clinton and Barack Obama disorganized the country of Libya by fueling the deposition of Muammar Gaddafi without thinking about what they were going to do next.) A common retort to Trump's early-morning tweets is that at least he, unlike Clinton, is actually up early. (She couldn't be bothered to be awoken while an embassy burned; it was, after all, only 90 percent of her job to ensure that our foreign policy was effectively carried out and our embassies and consulates were protected.)

But this book is not about Obama or Clinton, although they will be mentioned throughout this book to help provide the correct context for understanding Trump. No, instead this book is about two great men, Churchill and Trump, who saved Western

---

[33] Hourly History, *Winston Churchill: A Life from Beginning to End*, Amazon. com, 1.

[34] *Trump: How to Get Rich*, 194–209.

civilization in their time from massive threats. This book can serve many purposes, depending on the reader.

I hope supporters of President Trump can use this book as a resource for convincing friends, family, and neighbors to support him in the 2020 election, as well as to defend his reputation even after the election (shameless plug: I'm available to speak to groups about Trump and Churchill).

For those who are unsure about President Trump but at least have enough interest in learning more to pick up this book, I hope you see this book as a wonderful guide and an examination of how President Trump and Prime Minister Churchill are similar in many ways. Perhaps you don't agree with President Trump on every issue: on the tweeting, on the bluster, on his coarse language. Fair enough. But you will hopefully take two thoughts away from this book. First, Trump was made for a time like this, to save the U.S. for Western civilization. That is not to instill in him a Christ-like quality; others theoretically could have saved us but lacked the fortitude or courage to do so, as we will also see in this book. The second thought is, those very things about Trump that might give you pause are ultimately incredibly valuable in his fight to save this country.

I hope historians and admirers of Churchill can use this book as a new way to look at the historical legacy of Churchill and President Trump. Perhaps you will use this book to write your own book about Trump and Churchill, or to compare Trump to other past historical leaders. Maybe you will make your class buy this book so you can mock it.

This book looks at the legacies of Churchill and Trump through a variety of lenses: genius, plod, boldly grasping a moment, patriotism, and many other areas. It is best read all the way through, but you can certainly skip around from chapter to chapter as you wish. Throughout the book, I make ample use of quotes, anecdotes, and the writings of historians, biographers, and contemporary political commentators. I do so because I believe a good book has data and sources to back it up when possible, and I want to show that what I am arguing is not just the ramblings of a Trump supporter, and that it is based in fact.

If you are a conservative Republican, you can of course start off by assuming I have a bias toward Trump or have rose-colored vision regarding the president. No doubt, I strongly support most of what this president does. However, throughout the book, I will often acknowledge the criticism of President Trump, while offering rebuttals and explanations. No historian or writer is 100 percent neutral, but I do believe I have done a good job of acknowledging faults while also supporting our great president. With no reason to avoid controversy, let us now start with one way Trump and Churchill can be compared, and how they both saved Western civilization during their time: genius.

1

GENIUS

What is genius? It takes genius to be a defender of Western civilization. Churchill should be considered the first great defender of Western civilization. We can view him as inheriting Western civilization from a broad spectrum of thinkers, including Thomas Jefferson, James Madison, John Locke, and Edmund Burke, among others. These men do not have to agree on everything to more or less exemplify the beauties inherent in Western civilization. Genius is not necessarily being an academic or having a certain academic pedigree. Rather, it is a mix of knowledge and wisdom. A good diplomat, for example, must certainly know about the culture and history of the country he is assigned to, but he must also know how to work the entrepreneurs, politicians, and religious leaders there. He does not have to be learned on every type of food or whether the forty-seventh monarch of the country was Queen Elizabeth the Fifteenth or Queen Elizabeth the Sixteenth; rather, he must know how to work with the stakeholders and be able to know enough history and culture to identify with them to show he cares.

This is very much how Trump is a genius: he learns enough about what he needs to know, but more than anything, he understands *people* and what *people want*, having surely read or studied negotiation tactics at the Wharton School or learned from advisers to his businesses. And if he has never read a book about negotiation, then he is even more impressive because he sure as hell understands negotiation. This is something people did not grasp when Trump talked about being able to make a deal in the Middle East with Israel and Palestine. He did not have to have a degree in Middle Eastern studies to know the basics: Palestine views Israel as an occupier, Israel knows that Palestine is run by a terrorist group called Hamas, and both sides believe they have a historical and biblical claim to the land. Got it. Simplistic? Yes. Basically this covered the issue enough for Trump to start figuring out a way to broker some sort of deal? Yes. It's similar to North Korea: hates freedom, wants nukes; we want the country to have freedom and not have nukes. Great, let's get started.

I would argue that genius is not being the most well-read person in the room or someone who would win at a game of trivia. Genius must also contain emotional intelligence or interpersonal intelligence, the ability to read a room, to read a situation. We can think of it as a combination of knowing *enough* to be able to stake a position and make an argument and knowing *how* to package that argument to the right people. In considering this definition, we find that Churchill and Trump are geniuses. Now, for those in the mainstream media who actually did pick up this book (and kudos to you), calm down.

I'm sure your Twitter was running all night long after Trump said he was a "very stable genius."[35] Trump and Churchill are geniuses. It takes a genius to become the greatest defender of Western civilization. Let's start with how Trump is a genius.

For all the criticism that Trump is obtuse or lacks social grace, he has an incredible amount of interpersonal and emotional intelligence. You don't become the greatest developer in the New York real estate market by being a quiet fellow who works from 9:00 a.m. to 5:00 p.m. You become the greatest real estate developer by working long hours, but also by getting to know your clients and the people working for you. Trump is known to talk to everyone working for him as well as his guests. The laborer, the foreman, the bellhop. He does this first of all because he is a genuine guy and treats the little guy with respect. But he also does this because this is how he acquires the necessary knowledge to make decisions. Like the detective who becomes best friends with a local bartender, Trump knows who has the knowledge that others may not have or that others may not tell him.

The day laborer who is being sent home early every day is able to tell Trump, explicitly or not, that the supervisor isn't planning the construction schedule well, so people are running out of work to do during the day. The bellhop hears the complaints, or compliments, about guests' stays at a hotel while he is helping them pack up their cab to head to the airport and can relay that information to Trump so changes can be made. In fact, one of the criticisms of President Trump is that he has too

---

[35] Daniella Diaz, "Trump: 'I'm a 'very stable genius,'" CNN, January 6, 2018, https://www.cnn.com/2018/01/06/politics/donald-trump-white-house-fitness-very-stable-genius/index.html.

many people with too many beliefs feeding him information. Which is an odd criticism to make for people who *love* the concept of a "team of rivals" when it applies to Lincoln and anyone else. For Trump, his genius comes from knowing that the more liberal members of his inner circle, such as Ivanka Trump and Jared Kushner, may know some things that Sean Hannity or Rush Limbaugh doesn't, and vice versa. But he is able to take all these ideas and make a decision. He then has the emotional intelligence and genius to be able to read the room, so to speak, and calibrate as necessary.

In *Trump: How to Get Rich*, he explains that a leader must be honest and decisive: "If you equivocate, it's an indication you're unsure of yourself and what you're doing. It's also what politicians do all the time, and I find it inappropriate, insulting, and condescending."[36] This is a philosophy Trump carried with him into the White House. And as the president, he makes sure to listen to many people, to speak the truth, and to be open about what he believes, but also to be open to other ideas. He has demonstrated an amazing ability to feel the pulse of America and has used that to help all of us.

This translates into defending Western civilization because Trump is able to use that genius to deliver messages that resonate with people. If a typical politician started talking about "needing to make necessary security investments in our immigration system in order to stabilize the flow of illegal immigrants," your head would pop off by the fourth word. That's why Trump is successful; he keeps it short. Build. The. Wall. Bomb. The. Shit. Out. Of. ISIS. Not "work toward establishing a

---

[36] *Trump: How to Get Rich*, 17.

comprehensive military intervention or overseas contingency operation to reduce the functioning ability of a JV squad." No. Bomb the shit out of ISIS. That takes genius. Of course, having to reduce one's thoughts to 140 characters year after year is good training for becoming an effective communicator. Trump also knows that much of his base, as is typical for a Republican politician, are middle-aged, married men and women. So what did Trump, whose genius for tabloids and media was shaped as a real estate developer and New York socialite, do? He merged the political ideology of his daughter and son-in-law, pushing criminal justice reform with an entity who is popular and well known to millennials: Kim Kardashian. Oh, and did you remember that Kim Kardashian's stepparent, who is transgender, supported Trump? And now the media is forced to cover Trump's middle-ground beliefs on transgender people with his criminal-justice-reform measure. I mean, Trump was able to turn someone famous for a sex tape into a serious political advocate, who is now studying law. For bringing respectability to the Kardashian family once again, the man deserves a Nobel Peace Prize. That takes genius.

While the mainstream media do not consider Trump a genius, it is likely because they themselves don't realize how they are actually being carefully played by him. He forces them to cover news stories and forces them to reveal their innate hatred and hypocrisy. Normally, for example, the mainstream media are antiwar, but it's been suspected that they are antiwar only when Republicans are president. Trump's actions led to this revelation, when the mainstream media hounded Trump for considering bombing Iran and then criticized him for being indecisive when he called off the bombing at the last minute.

Churchill exercised great genius as well. He also did so through his words, knowing when to employ the proper emotions to make his argument. Consider these lines from one of his more famous speeches, in front of the House of Commons in 1940:

> I would say to the House, as I said to those who have joined this Government, I have nothing to offer but blood, toil, tears and sweat. We have before us an ordeal of the most grievous kind. We have before us many long months of toil and struggle.
>
> You ask what is our policy. I will say, it is to wage war with all our might, with all the strength that God can give us, to wage war against a monstrous tyranny never surpassed in the dark, lamentable catalogue of human crime.
>
> You ask what is our aim? I can answer in one word: Victory. Victory at all costs. Victory in spite of all terror. Victory however long and hard the road may be. For without victory there is no survival.[37]

"For without victory there is no survival." I repeat this phrase because it must be emphasized. It can be seen as one slogan that would aptly describe the leadership of both Trump and Churchill. President Trump's slogan is "Make America Great Again," like Churchill made England great again. But Trump is also making Western civilization safe again from the threats to its values.

When weak leaders like Obama are confronted with a problem, a nuclear Iran for example, their default decision is to run

---

[37] International Churchill Society, Famous Quotes and Stories—"No One Would Do Such Things," https://winstonchurchill.org/resources/quotes/famous-quotations-and-stories/.

away or to hand over the keys to the kingdom, so to speak, to the people they are afraid of. This is what Obama did when he let radical Islamic leaders in Iran write the terms of Iran's nuclear enrichment program, or when he let socialist French bureaucrats and Chinese business leaders work hand in hand to write the disastrous antifreedom, anti-American Paris Accords, once again allowing foreign governments to circumvent our American system of checks and balances. But Trump realized, as did Churchill, that giving in to outside forces is not true survival; true survival requires victory. A victorious negotiator in Iran would have used all the power we had to bring Iran to its knees and force it to stop enriching uranium for its nuclear program. A weak, cowardly leader like Obama, or Neville Chamberlain, believes in winning by not dying, whereas strong leaders like Trump and Churchill believe surviving means the ability to continue to set one's own destiny. "Better to die on your feet than to live on your knees" is the philosophy that describes Trump's and Churchill's genius leadership.

A good leader does not sugarcoat the truth, nor does he scare people into submission. Rather, he mixes the right amount of truth, urgency, and optimism to rally people to his side. In his speech, Churchill evoked, purposely or not, the imagery of Pericles's Funeral Oration, in which Pericles laments the loss of life in battle while making the argument that those people served a greater purpose, and that the families of the dead should be honored.

> *To you who are the sons and brothers of the departed, I see that the struggle to emulate them will be an arduous one. For all men praise the dead, and, however preeminent your*

*virtue may be, I do not say even to approach them, and avoid
living their rivals and detractors, but when a man is out of the
way, the honor and goodwill which he receives is unalloyed.
And, if I am to speak of womanly virtues to those of you who
will henceforth be widows, let me sum them up in one short
admonition: To a woman not to show more weakness than is
natural to her sex is a great glory, and not to be talked about
for good or for evil among men.*[38]

As we can see, Churchill was a genius at using rhetoric
and examples to prove his point. In his words and actions, he
inspired people by reminding them that as a nation, they had
to be united to root out evil. That's why phrases like "our sons
and brothers" and "our policy" were used: to send the idea and
reinforce the point that what Churchill did was ultimately for
and with the people of England. Therefore, the people felt like
Churchill had their best interests at heart and could trust him.
As noted earlier, this is a key part of genius: understanding people's emotions and how they think, so policy and rhetoric can
be shaped to rally support and to show support for one's country. Trump is also skilled at this.

Trump speaks with similar reverence when he speaks of
our brave veterans, and also when criticizing the foreign policy
blunders made by members of the foreign policy Establishment
who keep getting us into overseas wars without an exit strategy so that their buddies in the military-industrial complex can
continue to get rich on the blood of brave American patriots.

---

[38] "Thucydides, Pericles' Funeral Oration," University of Minnesota Human
Rights Library, http://hrlibrary.umn.edu/education/thucydides.html.

Despite this, I must continue to remind everyone of the assaults that Trump faced while running for office and that he faces as president, including frequent attacks on the ideals of Western civilization.

This is from the *National Catholic Register*, reporting on Amy Coney Barrett's confirmation fight:

> *The Democrat senator from California, Dianne Feinstein, attacked Barrett, a Catholic law professor at Notre Dame, with the accusation that she is essentially unfit for service as a federal judge because of her deeply held religious beliefs. "You are controversial," Feinstein declared. "You have a long history of believing that your religious beliefs should prevail." The Senator then added what has already become one of the most incendiary and widely repeated comments in recent memory: "When you read your speeches, the conclusion one draws is that the dogma lives loudly within you," Feinstein said. "And that's of concern when you come to big issues that large numbers of people have fought for years in this country."*[39]

U.S. senator Bernie Sanders, a man who read *The Gulag Archipelago* and thought it was a book praising the Soviet Union (probably), carried out a relentless and anti-American attack on Russ Vought. Vought, an accomplished Christian conservative, was nominated for the Office of Management and Budget and was attacked by Sanders for a previous theological statement he had made about Muslims, which was in no way inflammatory and was a simply stated Christian belief. The exchange was

---

[39] Matthew Bunson, "Sen. Feinstein Grills Catholic Nominee: 'The Dogma Lives Loudly within You,'" *National Catholic Register*, September 7, 2017, http://www.ncregister.com/blog/mbunson/sen.-feinstein-grills-catholic-nominee-the-dogma-lives-loudly-within-you.

so bad that even the liberal *Atlantic* took issue with Sanders's bigotry, writing, "Article VI of the U.S. Constitution states that 'no religious test shall ever be required as a qualification to any office or public trust under the United States.' On Wednesday, Senator Bernie Sanders flirted with the boundaries of this rule during a confirmation hearing for Russell Vought, President Trump's nominee for deputy director of the Office of Management and Budget."[40]

Other leftists also carried out anti-American, anti-religious attacks on Trump's nominees. For example, the prominent charity and Catholic organization the Knights of Columbus found itself under attack in a way that was completely unacceptable. Federal judge Brian Buescher faced attacks from Senator Kamala Harris and Senator Mazie Hirono over his membership. *Newsweek* reports:

> *The Knights of Columbus, the world's largest Catholic fraternal organization, accused Democratic Senators Kamala Harris and Mazie Hirono of invoking America's anti-Catholic history in their questioning of a judicial nominee about his membership to the club.*
>
> *The senators directed a series of questions to Brian Buescher, President Donald Trump's nominee for the U.S. District Court in the District of Nebraska, about how his membership with the service organization might affect his decisions as a federal judge.*

---

[40] Emma Green, "Bernie Sanders's Religious Test for Christians in Public Office," *The Atlantic*, June 8, 2017, https://www.theatlantic.com/politics/archive/2017/06/bernie-sanders-chris-van-hollen-russell-vought/529614/.

This attack was so vicious and unethical that the Knights of Columbus had to respond by pointing out the obvious: "Our country's sad history of anti-Catholic bigotry contributed to the founding of the Knights of Columbus, and we are proud of the many Catholics who overcame this hurdle to contribute so greatly to our country."[41]

The best part of Trump's strategy was that he picked highly qualified, respected people to be nominated, forcing the Democrats to make ridiculous arguments. Another way Trump's nominee strategy reflected his genius was that these nomination fights necessarily forced the media to cover the Middle America appeal of his nominees. A regular Catholic guy. A Catholic professor who teaches at Notre Dame. A Christian who holds firm to his beliefs but is respectful of other religions. Trump nominated Linda McMahon, a World Wrestling Entertainment executive, for example; wrestling is popular in the heartland. In other words, he picked successful but regular people to be his nominees.

History is replete with examples of great leaders who used genius to rally the troops, so to speak. To win people over to their side. A good leader must employ genius to defend civilization from threats, otherwise he allows it to spread like a virus. This is much the situation Trump came into in 2017 and what Churchill came into after Chamberlain; the leader before each of these two great men had been weak and tried to hide the truth and deceive his own people, so as not to scare them or, we

---

[41] Nicole Goodkind, "Democrats Accused of 'Anti-Catholic Bigotry' by Knights of Columbus over Trump Judicial Nominee Questioning,'" *Newsweek*, December 24, 2018, https://www.newsweek.com/democrats-catholic-bigotry-trump-knights-columbus-1270859.

can assume, reveal his own fear and lack of good judgment. In both cases, it took a genius, as described in this chapter, to clean up the mess and win back the trust of the people.

Showing the genius of Trump in playing the media, TheStreet reports:

> Donald Trump didn't spend nearly as much on advertising as typical presidential candidates, and he didn't have to—he relied on billions of dollars of free mentions in media ranging from major TV news networks to Buzzfeed and Twitter instead.... Over the past 12 months, the president-elect received more than $800 million in free earned broadcast media, compared to $666 million for Clinton, and $2.6 billion in free earned online news attention, compared to $1.6 billion for his rival. He edged out her and other major political names in American and worldwide newspapers as well.[42]

So the media hate Trump, but Trump is such a genius that he actually got them to give him free coverage—which led him into the White House.

To summarize, a genius is able to use knowledge and interpersonal intelligence to get his agenda implemented and to lead people. Both Churchill and Trump demonstrated a keen ability to do this throughout their time in office.

---

[42] Emily Stewart, "Donald Trump Rode $5 Billion in Free Media to the White House," TheStreet, November 20, 2016, https://www.thestreet.com/story/13896916/1/donald-trump-rode-5-billion-in-free-media-to-the-white-house.html.

2

PLOD

"Success is not final, failure is not fatal: it is the courage to continue that counts."

—WINSTON CHURCHILL

Plod is the ability to keep fighting when everything is against you. In many ways, plod is the only thing that keeps a society going, since it is the will to fight and the energy to not give up in the fight for what is right and true.

Plod has been reflected in both Churchill and Trump, and is what aided them in defending Western civilization from its enemies. It means that even when the odds seemed stacked against them or society, they were able to keep society going and rally the troops.

For example, Churchill exemplified plod in one of his famous speeches, in which he literally rallied the troops. In this speech, Churchill took one victory and made sure to keep people focused on the long-term prize. As the International Churchill Society writes:

> Churchill's "We shall fight on the beaches" speech on 4 June 1940 is a eulogy to the British war effort that has been immortalised in popular memory of the Second World War. As a newly appointed Prime Minister, Churchill's first month in office was defined by the Dunkirk evacuation. Over 300,000 Allied soldiers were evacuated in a sensational rescue mission. The success was down to a combination of German errors and the brilliant execution of the evacuation plan. However, the fact remained that, with France now fallen, Britain had become an attractive target for German invasion. In this speech, Churchill's aim was to counter the jubilant public reaction provoked by the evacuation from Dunkirk, and bring the discussion back to reality. As Churchill famously warns in the speech, "We must be very careful not to assign to this deliverance the attributes of a victory. Wars are not won by evacuations."[43]

To help set the stage, the people of England were excited that a massive military undertaking had been successful. But as Churchill made sure to remind them, more perseverance would be necessary in order to achieve the ultimate goal of crushing fascist totalitarianism. Below I've included some of my favorite lines from the speech, but I do encourage you to read the whole speech. I've punctuated each section with some commentary to explain what is being said and how it fits the idea of plod.

---

[43] International Churchill Society, "Fight Them on the Beaches, 4 June 1940," https://winstonchurchill.org/resources/speeches/1940-the-finest-hour/fight-them-on-the-beaches/.

But it certainly seemed that the whole of the French First Army and the whole of the British Expeditionary Force north of the Amiens-Abbeville gap would be broken up in the open field or else would have to capitulate for lack of food and ammunition. These were the hard and heavy tidings for which I called upon the House and the nation to prepare themselves a week ago. The whole root and core and brain of the British Army, on which and around which we were to build, and are to build, the great British Armies in the later years of the war, seemed about to perish upon the field or to be led into an ignominious and starving captivity.

In this part, Churchill is setting the stage for Parliament to understand the situation they were facing. Not one to paper over problems, Churchill makes it clear that the entire history and legacy of the famed British Army were on the line during Dunkirk, either through being killed or having to surrender.

We must be very careful not to assign to this deliverance the attributes of a victory. Wars are not won by evacuations. But there was a victory inside this deliverance, which should be noted. It was gained by the Air Force. Many of our soldiers coming back have not seen the Air Force at work; they saw only the bombers which escaped its protective attack. They underrate its achievements. I have heard much talk of this; that is why I go out of my way to say this. I will tell you about it.

Here, Churchill is explaining the crux of his speech, which is that the successful evacuation is just one of many battles that will have to be fought in the overall war.

May it not also be that the cause of civilization itself will be defended by the skill and devotion of a few thousand airmen? There never has been, I suppose, in all the world, in all the history of war, such an opportunity for youth. The Knights of the Round Table, the Crusaders, all fall back into the past— not only distant but prosaic; these young men, going forth every morn to guard their native land and all that we stand for, holding in their hands these instruments of colossal and shattering power...

This part is very interesting, because it ties directly into how Churchill saw the war: as a battle for civilization. He praises and points out that the British military is made up of young people, and that young people must continue to join and fight.

I have, myself, full confidence that if all do their duty, if nothing is neglected, and if the best arrangements are made, as they are being made, we shall prove ourselves once again able to defend our Island home, to ride out the storm of war, and to outlive the menace of tyranny, if necessary for years, if necessary alone. At any rate, that is what we are going to try to do. That is the resolve of His Majesty's Government—every man of them. That is the will of Parliament and the nation. The British Empire and the French Republic, linked together in their cause and in their need, will defend to the death their native soil, aiding each other like good comrades to the utmost of their strength. Even though large tracts of Europe and many old and famous States have fallen or may fall into the grip of the Gestapo and all the odious apparatus of Nazi rule, we shall not flag or fail.

This is a good reminder that the British people were ready to fight until the death at the side of their ally France.

We shall go on to the end, we shall fight in France, we shall fight on the seas and oceans, we shall fight with growing confidence and growing strength in the air, we shall defend our Island, whatever the cost may be, we shall fight on the beaches, we shall fight on the landing grounds, we shall fight in the fields and in the streets, we shall fight in the hills; we shall never surrender, and even if, which I do not for a moment believe, this Island or a large part of it were subjugated and starving, then our Empire beyond the seas, armed and guarded by the British Fleet, would carry on the struggle, until, in God's good time, the New World, with all its power and might, steps forth to the rescue and the liberation of the old.[44]

This speech is one of my favorites and one of Churchill's most famous speeches. It is a rallying cry for the military, for Parliament, for the country, and for the Allied forces. Churchill is clear on the idea that the people must continue to fight and plod along in order to defend the great history of their people.

President Trump would echo similar themes on the campaign trail and as a president, making clear that as a united country, the United States would never be defeated. As I did with Churchill, we will now look at the words of Trump to see how his rhetoric encouraged disenchanted and discouraged people.

One of the best examples of this would be Trump's inaugural speech. For those who may be reading this book after Trump is out of office, it's worth pointing out that as I write this, Trump's presidency is contentious, and even though numerous

---

[44] International Churchill Society, "We Shall Fight on the Beaches, June 4, 1940," https://winstonchurchill.org/resources/speeches/1940-the-finest-hour/we-shall-fight-on-the-beaches/.

lawsuits and wild theories claiming that Trump didn't really win have been dismissed and discredited, some people are still bitter over his election.

In his 2017 inauguration speech,[45] Trump used similar language to rally and unite people around a common cause. In this section, I'll again pick out some of my favorite parts. At the end of this book I include the full speech; I strongly suggest reading it through and using it to arm yourself against the lies and hatred of leftists who don't appreciate our president.

> *We, the citizens of America, are now joined in a great national effort to rebuild our country and to restore its promise for all of our people. Together, we will determine the course of America and the world for years to come.*
>
> *We will face challenges. We will confront hardships. But we will get the job done.*

In the opening, Trump sets a positive tone, saying that the people of the country will rebuild and things will be better. He also acknowledges that there are problems they face, but they "will get the job done."

> *For too long, a small group in our nation's Capital has reaped the rewards of government while the people have borne the cost. Washington flourished—but the people did not share in its wealth. Politicians prospered—but the jobs left, and the factories closed. The establishment protected itself, but not the citizens of our country. Their victories have not been your victories; their triumphs have not been your triumphs; and*

---

[45]   Donald J. Trump, "The Inaugural Address," January 20, 2017, whitehouse. gov, https://www.whitehouse.gov/briefings-statements/the-inaugural-address/.

while they celebrated in our nation's Capital, there was little to celebrate for struggling families all across our land. That all changes—starting right here, and right now, because this moment is your moment: it belongs to you.

In this part of the speech, Trump rips into the corrupt Establishment and the globalists who sold out American interests on behalf of making more money. Trump sends a clear and powerful message to downtrodden Americans who are sick of the bipartisan racket of politics and just want an opportunity to realize the American dream. This is where he goes to in the next part of this speech.

But for too many of our citizens, a different reality exists: Mothers and children trapped in poverty in our inner cities; rusted-out factories scattered like tombstones across the landscape of our nation; an education system, flush with cash, but which leaves our young and beautiful students deprived of knowledge; and the crime and gangs and drugs that have stolen too many lives and robbed our country of so much unrealized potential. This American carnage stops right here and stops right now. We are one nation—and their pain is our pain. Their dreams are our dreams; and their success will be our success. We share one heart, one home, and one glorious destiny. The oath of office I take today is an oath of allegiance to all Americans. We must protect our borders from the ravages of other countries making our products, stealing our companies, and destroying our jobs. Protection will lead to great prosperity and strength. I will fight for you with every breath in my body—and I will never, ever let you down. America will start winning again, winning like never before.

Here Trump is driving a stake into the lies and falsehoods of the Democratic Party, which lied to people in poverty and sold them out through unfair trade deals (with the help of Republicans) and kept people trapped in a permanent underclass, coming around only for votes. This is why Trump scares Democrats; he goes straight for the people they always take for granted and take advantage of. He makes clear that the people will plod along and fight the destructive big-government policies of Democrats.

We will reinforce old alliances and form new ones—and unite the civilized world against Radical Islamic Terrorism, which we will eradicate completely from the face of the Earth.

This is just a great part about fighting radical Islamic terrorism, which the weak and feckless Obama was afraid to name, partially because he was probably okay with the values of Western civilization's being stolen and pillaged by the tenets of sharia law.

When America is united, America is totally unstoppable. There should be no fear—we are protected, and we will always be protected. We will be protected by the great men and women of our military and law enforcement and, most importantly, we are protected by God.... Do not let anyone tell you it cannot be done. No challenge can match the heart and fight and spirit of America. We will not fail. Our country will thrive and prosper again. We stand at the birth of a new millennium, ready to unlock the mysteries of space, to free the Earth from the miseries of disease, and to harness the energies, industries and technologies of tomorrow.

"Plod" means being unstoppable and fighting on, and here Trump shows by rallying people that this is their time: America will come back; America will return to the days of glory and recover from the destructive policies of softness toward radical Islam, nation building, selling Americans out to the big banks and multinational corporations and political correctness. That is why (and note that these words are all capitalized in the speech)…

> *Together, We Will Make America Strong Again. We Will Make America Wealthy Again. We Will Make America Proud Again. We Will Make America Safe Again. And, Yes, Together, We Will Make America Great Again. Thank you, God Bless You, And God Bless America.*

In this chapter I've deviated from the formula used in much of the rest of the book, because one way that both Trump and Churchill kept their people plodding along was with their words; that's why it is so important that we examine what they said at key points in their leadership.

Now, with a greater understanding of how they think, we'll turn to how Trump and Churchill both boldly grasped the moment in front of them.

3

COINCIDENCE AND A MOMENT BOLDLY GRASPED

It takes a special man not only to notice a problem but also to heed the call to solve the problem. In this chapter, I want to talk about how Trump and Churchill were the right men for the right time. Those of faith may believe that God has made us for a time such as this, or that God qualifies the called. If you are not religious or do not agree with that view, that is okay too; we can all agree that both Prime Minister Churchill and President Trump boldly grasped the moment presented to them. In fact, this is one very important thing that is often lost in academia, in think tanks, and on everyone else inside the Beltway: Trump became president at a time when the world, including the U.S., was falling apart for many Americans. Many leftists fail to see this connection because they have never had to fear job loss; there has been a steady stream of taxpayer funding and George Soros money to keep them employed, so they create worthless and debunked papers about redistributing money or how we just need to try socialism one more time and it will work. The establishment politicians, the consultant class, or what Angelo Codevilla calls the ruling class, fails to grasp that average Americans have been struggling. Writing in his popular book, called *The Ruling Class*, during the first term of the Obama presidency, Codevilla makes this problem easy to understand.

> *Ever since the 1930s, as people who think this way have taken over more and more functions in an even bigger government, they have become ever more inclined to dismiss the public's opposition as ignorant, and to believe themselves entitled to shape a new and different America. Through their conception of their own superiority, and by accumulating power, they have made themselves into a bipartisan Ruling Class that now dominates public affairs and encroaches ever more into our lives' most intimate details.... From Atlanta to Seattle, today's Ruling Class was exposed to a narrow, uniform set of ideas, and adopted a set of habits and tastes, as well as a secular canon of sacred myths, saints, sins and ritual language. The class' chief pretention is its intellectual superiority: its members claim to know things that the common herd cannot.*[46]

In other words, those in the ruling class believe:

▶ Whatever they now say is true must be true. Two genders become five hundred. Global cooling becomes global warming becomes climate change.

---

[46] Angelo M. Codevilla, *The Ruling Class: How They Corrupted America and What We Can Do about It* (New York: Beaufort Books, 2010), xvii–xix.

- ▶ They know more than others do; they went to Georgetown or Harvard after all!

- ▶ All Trump supporters are poor people who don't know what's good for them—they are "deplorables"—but simultaneously, all Trump supporters are also wealthy people who support Trump because he will let them destroy the country in pursuit of their own wealth.

As we can see, this is how the ruling class looks at us and President Trump.

Both President Trump and Winston Churchill had the challenge and opportunity, depending on how you view life, to come after an ineffectual and weak leader, one who kowtowed to political correctness; their predecessors were weak, weak men (although history books don't note it, we can assume that Neville Chamberlain would have worn "mom jeans" too, had jeans been in fashion in England at the time) and put their own political legacy above the safety and prosperity of their country. Brash and unafraid, President Trump spent most of the Obama presidency correctly criticizing Obama for his weakness on issues like trade, China, and radical Islam, and for playing into the media's hand by supporting falsehoods about police officers' killing unarmed black men. Writing in *The Case for Trump*, Victor Davis Hanson explains, "After 2008, Democrats were increasingly candid in voicing socialist bromides...open borders, identity politics, higher taxes, more government regulation, free college tuition, single-payer government-run health care...and a European Union–like foreign policy [open borders, 'tolerance' for Islamic immigrants who don't share Western values, etc.]."[47] The bold decisions of Churchill and Trump in grasping the moment, as well as a bit of luck at having the opportunity to do so, are why they will be remembered as the defenders of Western civilization.

Likewise, Chamberlain famously wanted "peace in our time," which ultimately led to destruction in our time, the Holocaust, the Soviet Union, and problems in Europe that continue to this day. For this, we can say that Churchill and Trump lived in the right time for them to lead, but they also boldly grasped the situation. It was they who boldly took the steps to right the ship, even though there were, theoretically, others who could have, but lacked the fortitude to do so. A good defender of his family, his country, his society, or Western civilization steps in where others fear to tread. A true leader, whether Churchill or Trump, boldly defends those most in need, without regard to what others' fears are. As will be demonstrated throughout this book, both Churchill and Trump have the endearing qualities of being able step in where others are afraid, but also to lead boldly and recognize the problems that got their people to where they are. To use a construction analogy apt for President Trump, you cannot make buildings better without first recognizing the flaws in buildings that have fallen. As a real estate developer, Trump learned the skills necessary to be president: listen to the people, study a problem, make a decision, and then be open to seeing how your decision plays out and adjust accordingly.

One of Trump's most endearing qualities, and one that makes him a defender of Western civilization, is his ability to make decisions, to take advice but ultimately not worry what

---

[47] Victor Davis Hanson, *The Case for Trump* (New York: Basic Books, 2019), 4.

critics who are clearly always going to be critics will say. He is actually known for taking advice from a wide variety of people, then putting it all together and making a decision. What he does not do, and this benefits us all, is worry about what the mainstream media or leftist professors or think tanks will say about his decisions. Rather, he views a variety of his advisers as representing the common people and what they will say about his views; for example, he should be praised for giving voices to liberal but reasonable people like Jared Kushner and Ivanka Trump. They represent old-school liberals who are concerned about true matters of fairness and justice in issues such as labor, criminal justice, and economic opportunity. They are not politically correct monsters seeking to impose a nefarious vision on the world; rather, they represent a liberal point of view, but one that does still ultimately care about the human person and his situation.

Trump lays this philosophy out in *Trump: How to Get Rich*: "People can offer an interesting mix of pros and cons. Time will do the weeding out for you. All you have to do is pay attention. What I look for in employees is a sense of responsibility that goes beyond merely sufficient. Some people do the bare minimum, and some people will actually be concerned about the organization as a whole."[48]

This is a wonderful way of looking at the world. Trump does not want someone who does "good enough for government" work (probably one reason the Establishment complex of public-sector employee union leadership and lazy government employees hates him, while the hard workers do not); he

---

[48] Trump: *How to Get Rich*, 24.

wants someone who wants to make things better and wants to improve the organization throughout.

Codevilla has written extensively of the problems with entrenched interests in government, some of which now can be considered part of the deep state—the people working overtime (well, not real overtime of course; they're government workers after all) to stop President Trump's agenda, because they don't want to see radical Islam stopped (that would mean less money for the military-industrial complex), they don't want to see a free-market energy system (that would mean fewer jobs for the solar-panel-awareness subdepartment of the Department of Energy's committee on saving the environment), and they definitely don't want to see a reduction in the size and scope of government.

Codevilla lays out the problems in *The Ruling Class*. Here is some of what he has to say:

> ▶ "Our rulers believe it is right for the ruled to shut up
> and obey, or at most cut little deals for themselves.
> The ruled believe they have a God-given right to
> self-governance.... The Ruling Class' proximate objec-
> tives—allowing only such economic activities as are
> part of its plans, finishing the transformation of Amer-
> ica into an administrative state, reducing American
> families to Swedish levels of intellectual and moral
> subordination to government 'science' of all sources
> of reason or authority—are based on its claim of supe-
> riority and its denigration of lower beings, which it
> shouts from the housetops."[49]

---

[49] *Ruling Class*, 67.

▶ "The bureaucrats' powers to tell us what kinds of light bulbs or cars we can use, or how many hoops we must jump through before doing any number of things, derive from laws, each of which is based on the same premise: ordinary people, as consumers, landowners, or citizens, are incompetent to make such decisions."[50]

One thing Trump has been able to do amazingly well is take on the entrenched leaders and not buy into the go-along-to-get-along mentality. In fact, Trump has swiftly moved to punish the awful people who used to work in the Veterans Administration, by making it easier for incompetent federal employees to be fired. This is something that good federal employees, of which there are many, supported because it made their jobs more valuable; it brought honor back to what it means to work for the federal government. Of course the Establishment public-sector unions, which exist to bleed the taxpayer dry of hard-earned money earned in the private, productive sector, predictably opposed this. Nevertheless, Trump persisted.

This is a valuable trait that is not seen in every leader. Churchill too exemplified this, not as an employee but as a leader. Sometimes he had to stand out from the others who just wanted to go along to get along, but in his case we're not talking about an employee at an average company; we're talking about the fate of Western civilization and Europe as we know it.

William Manchester sets the scene so eloquently for one way in which Churchill oftentimes stood alone. Writing in *Defender of the Realm*, the third volume of his *Last Lion* biography of Churchill, Manchester notes:

---

[50] *Ruling Class*, 71.

On June 21, 1940, the first day of summer, Winston Churchill was the most visible man in England. France accepted Hitler's surrender terms that day and, with virtually all of Europe now under the swastika, with the Soviet Union a Nazi accomplice, and the United States isolationist, Britain and the Dominions confronted the Third Reich alone. Prime minister for only six weeks, Churchill was defending more than his island home.... The gravity of his role was obvious.... He was a multifarious individual, including within one man a whole troupe of characters, some of them subversive of one another and none feigned.[51]

To put it another way, Churchill was in charge of defending not just England but the whole of Europe and Western civilization, other European countries either having surrendered or willingly joined forces with totalitarian powers, while the United States sat on the sidelines. It would be Churchill alone who could boldly fight back against evil forces. In 1939, Churchill spoke out against totalitarianism and against Nazi Germany, seeing what was going on a month before the Second World War started. He said this in his praise of democratic institutions and in criticism of Nazi Germany:

The architects of the American Constitution were as careful as those who shaped the British Constitution, to guard against the whole life and fortunes, and all the laws and freedom of the nation, being places in the hands of a tyrant. Checks and counter-checks in the body politic, large devolutions of State government, instruments and processes of free debate,

---

[51] William Manchester and Paul Reid, *The Last Lion: Winston Spencer Churchill—Defender of the Realm, 1940–1965* (Boston: Little, Brown, 2012), 3.

*frequent recurrence to first principles, the right of opposition
to the most powerful governments, and above all ceaseless
vigilance, have preserved, and will preserve, the broad characteristics of British and American institutions.*

(We can see this in Trump's support of the Second Amendment.)

These, Churchill argues, are the positive developments in
Western civilization that have preserved liberty and allowed
a free society to endure. He points out, "But in Germany, on
a mountain peak, there sits one man, who in a single day can
release the world from the fear which now oppresses it; or, in
a single day can plunge all that we have are into a volcano of
smoke and flame."[52] No one man should have this much power,
and the Germans failed the world by allowing Hitler to rise up
the way he did and seize the nation and then cause worldwide
strife through his horrible and deplorable actions and ideology. Interestingly, while Hitler's life had led him to this point
of being a fascist, racist dictator, Churchill too, it seemed, had
been spending his life preparing to take down a dictator (or two),
and totalitarianism at large, if the moment called him to do so.

In his great book *Churchill: Walking with Destiny*, Andrew
Roberts quotes Charles Eade, a newspaper editor, in explaining
that Churchill felt that he had spent his whole life preparing to
boldly seize a moment, to be a wartime prime minister. Eade
says, as related by Roberts: "He explained to me that he was
able to handle all these affairs at the centre, because his whole
life had been a training for the high office he had filled during
the war." Quoting Churchill: "I felt as if I were walking with

---

[52]   *Churchill: The Power of Words*, 222.

destiny, and that all my past life had been but a preparation for this hour and for this trial." Churchill wrote this about becoming prime minister after Hitler had launched his blitzkrieg.[53] He knew that he had been shaped for a time such as this.

Similarly, William Manchester writes:

> Before England could fight she needed, not only troops and arms but also a government of fighting ministers, men prepared—as soldiers must be—to sacrifice everything, including their lives, toward a great objective, the destruction of Nazi Germany. Churchill was such a man. Despite his membership in the cabinet, however, he was virtually alone. The rest of the government was schizoid.[54]

In other words, Churchill knew he had to lead, and probably realized very quickly that he was going to be virtually alone. As the saying goes, if you want to lead the orchestra, you have to turn your back on the crowd. It was this ability to forge ahead, alone, that led Churchill to being seen by many as one of the greatest defenders of Western civilization.

In a speech less than a month after the one recently referenced, Churchill, who was still not prime minister, laid out for the House of Commons what was at stake (he had recently been named lord of admiralty by Neville Chamberlain, a position he had also served in from 1911 to 1915). He conveyed the utter importance of undertaking a war with Germany, and why the people must be prepared to fight. In this speech, we see the traits and skills that made him both a great defender of Western

---

[53] *Churchill: The Power of Words*, 2.
[54] William Manchester, *The Last Lion: Winston Spencer Churchill—Alone, 1932–1940* (Boston: Little, Brown, 1988), 582.

civilization and an excellent prime minister, the greatest England ever had.

Churchill explained that what they were defending was more than just a country; it was an idea, a way of life and, most broadly, freedom and liberty. Here's what he had to say:

This is of the highest moral value—and not only moral value, but practical value—at the present time, because the whole-hearted concurrence of scores of millions of men and women whose co-operation is indispensable and whose comradeship and brotherhood are indispensable, is the only foundation upon which the trial and tribulation of modern war can be endured and surmounted. This moral conviction alone affords the ever-fresh resilience which renews the strength and energy of people in long, doubtful, and dark days. Outside, the storms of war may blow and the lands may be lashed with the fury of its gales, but in our own hearts this Sunday morning there is peace. Our hands may be active, but our consciences are at rest.

He then explained that this was a monumental task, but one that England was prepared to take on. Churchill's speech is only a few paragraphs yet is so incredible that I must continue with it.

The Prime Minister said it was a sad day, and that is indeed true, but at the present time there is another note, which may be present, and that is a feeling of thankfulness that, if these great trials were to come upon our Island, there is a generation of Britons here now ready to prove itself not unworthy of the days of yore, and not unworthy of those great men, the fathers of our land, who laid the foundation of our laws and

*shaped the greatness of our country. This is not a question of
fighting for Danzig or fighting for Poland. We are fighting to
save the whole world from the pestilence of Nazi tyranny and
in defence of all that is most sacred to man.*[55]

President Trump has often had to go at it alone, including
venturing further into the real estate game in New York than his
father did. And given the nature of the real estate game, Trump
would have few friends in the industry, since his gain would be
largely everyone else's loss. And though the high-stakes game
of New York real estate is still not as pressure-filled as trying to
defeat Nazi Germany, Trump's skills in real estate helped make
him a great leader to defeat radical Islam.

Likewise, years of playing the New York media game, danc-
ing with the tabloid press, and battling through bankruptcy
and politicians prepared Trump for a time such as the one he
grabbed. What's the *Washington Post* editorial board to someone who came through a billion-dollar bankruptcy, multiple
divorces, and the New York political scene as a billionaire,
married to one of the most beautiful women in the world and
actually beloved by conservative Christian voters, whom many
assumed would be turned off by Trump's larger-than-life life-
style? Many voters were able to put aside their personal beliefs
because they saw that Trump could lead the country. In fact,
far from being hypocrites, conservative Christian voters were
actually being completely rational; their faith was something
they lived in their own lives, and it influenced their politics, but
at the end of the day their faith and values were not going to
be determined by a politician. A politician should lead morally,

---

[55]   *Churchill: The Power of Words.*

but not necessarily in the same way that leadership is viewed in religion.

For Trump, let's set the stage for the sort of situation he came into as president. President Obama was a weak leader, one who destroyed American health care by ramming through an unpopular government takeover, costing him many seats in the Senate and the House after only two years in office. Having created chaos in the U.S., he and Secretary Clinton—who should never be allowed anywhere near our nuclear arsenal, by the way—set out to "re-create" the Middle East, leading to turmoil in places like Libya. At least George W. Bush had a plan for when he deposed Middle Eastern dictators. Back on the domestic front, our police officers felt discouraged because President Obama took his talking points not from a clear and neutral reading of the situation in places like Ferguson, Missouri, but from Black Lives Matter activists and Al Sharpton. Similarly, third-rate quarterbacks were elevated to the MLKs of their day for kneeling on the field during the national anthem, which was truly a waste of the only chance they had to set foot on a football field in uniform, except perhaps to bring water to the starting quarterback. College campuses were overrun with political correctness, as triggered snowflakes called everything racist and leftist professors preached hatred for America and American values.

For example:

▶ A professor compared the libertarian group Young Americans for Liberty to a hate group just because it offered a free-speech ball on campus (basically a giant beach ball on which people could write whatever they wanted).[56]

▶ A journalism professor at the University of Missouri tried to get *a journalist* kicked out of a rally on campus against perceived injustices on campuses.[57]

▶ A professor in Denver forced students to recite a new Pledge of Allegiance that accused America of hating the poor, of homophobia, and of being anti-immigrant.[58]

Numerous professors wished Trump would be assassinated, or compared Trump to Hitler and/or Republicans to Nazis. Worse, the situation on campuses made our country unsafe, because criticizing radical Islam was seen as racist or xenophobic, a complete butchering of those terms, akin to the butchering of innocent Christians. Obama took the side of the politically correct crowd, allowing a so-called JV team to wreak havoc in the Middle East, a mess that Trump had to clean up, the same way that Chamberlain's softness toward Nazi Germany had to

[56] Max Diamond, Reed College, "Students Launch Libertarian Club at Small Oregon College and Get Harassed, Investigated, Condemned," The College Fix, June 21, 2017, https://www.thecollegefix.com/students-launch-libertarian-club-small-oregon-college-get-harassed-investigated-condemned/.

[57] Greg Piper, "Former Mizzou Professor Melissa Click Gets Contract Renewed at Gonzaga: 'She Has Excelled,'" September 14, 2017, https://www.thecollegefix.com/former-mizzou-professor-melissa-click-gets-contract-renewed-gonzaga-excelled/.

[58] "Professor Makes Students Recite 'Anti-American' Pledge of Allegiance," Fox News Insider, December 8, 2014, https://insider.foxnews.com/2014/12/08/metropolitan-state-university-professor-makes-students-recite-anti-american-pledge.

be cleaned up by the boldness of Churchill. It is ironic that professors who hate Trump never find the courage to call out actual
hatred and actual totalitarianism like that practiced by radical
Islamists and authoritarian Communists. It's far easier to call
someone a fascist or Nazi for supporting ideas like lowering the
corporate tax rate, protecting free-speech rights, or wanting to
protect women and babies from the violence of abortion. Better
to fight many windmills and say you won than to confront a real
dragon that you so desperately believe in, after all.

It is in fact in foreign policy where Trump has made the
strongest strides, despite this being the area where one would
expect him to have the least success as president. We would
expect a businessman and real estate developer to be able to
have a strong grasp on the basic economic issues at play—taxes,
regulations, labor concerns, and so on—and Trump by all mea-
sures has done a tremendous job of supercharging a moribund
economy. On social issues, he can more easily surround himself with key advisers and implement a standard Republican
social-issue agenda—enacting pro-life policies, appointing originalist judges, allowing the states and localities to set policies
with regard to discrimination and the "rights" of transgender
people. But with hundreds of countries, the European Union,
the United Nations, NATO, numerous trade agreements, and
an entrenched foreign-policy Establishment (the deep state)
to contend with, Trump could be forgiven if he were slower to
enact a new, populist foreign policy. But in fact, Trump boldly
seized the moment on foreign policy, and in doing so, truly put
America first! It in fact takes a brash Queens real estate developer to say no when presented with the argument that "we've

always done it this way" on issues of foreign policy. Here are just a few examples of his boldness.

Germany/NATO

The conventional wisdom of those who hold a master's degree in security studies from Georgetown, or the fellows at the Council on Foreign Relations, is that you cannot—nay, you *must not*—criticize NATO. Even though military alliances are meant to be that—alliances, fair agreements, equal partnerships—God forbid you even challenge whether or not someone is pulling his weight in the relationship, as if simply being in the partnership is enough weight-pulling (it is like being married and one person is doing all of the work to keep the marriage alive; the other spouse has fulfilled his or her commitment, the argument goes, simply by having said "I do" on the wedding day). But that's exactly what Donald Trump did and is doing as a candidate and as president—chastising countries for not fulfilling their contractual obligations regarding military forces. And for that, Trump is, of course, attacked and attacked and attacked. After all, how dare we attack our longstanding ally Germany (who was not our ally until the 1950s, but anyway). And the foreign policy Establishment is wrong.

Victor Davis Hanson, writing in *The Case for Trump*, notes, "Indeed, by 2018 a few formerly tightfisted NATO members were at least upping their commitments."[59] Of course, in their writings, the left-wing media oddly try to say that *doing exactly what Trump wants* is somehow *in defiance of Trump*. Writing

---

[59] *The Case for Trump*, 73.

for The Hill, Janusz Bugajski of K Street foreign policy think tank number 557 (oops, sorry, that's the Center for European Policy Analysis; I get them mixed up a lot) says:

> Trump threatened to cut American support if these targets were not met, claiming that American taxpayers should not bear the main burden for defending a wealthy Europe. Trump's words and Russia's threats have had an impact, with several capitals pledging to boost their spending and improve their fighting capabilities. NATO Secretary General Jens Stoltenberg recently asserted that Trump's demands have produced results: By the end of 2020, the allies will have added $100 billion to their defense budgets.[60]

The above appears in an op-ed that starts by questioning whether Trump wants NATO strengthened, and Bugajski muses that no matter what Trump wants, he has reinvigorated NATO by getting it to spend more on defense, *which is what Trump wants.* This is a theme we will see play out several times in trade as well: Trump uses bluster and social media to get our allies to play along with us, much to the surprise of the foreign policy Establishment and the left-wing media.

To the average voter who has to work sixty hours a week, or is retired and attending to the joys of retirement, negotiating trade isn't something that needs tenure or a doctorate to understand. The average voter sees a problem, a trade imbalance or unfair tariffs, and wants a solution. Trump delivers that solution: let's get to the table, let's talk, let's figure out this problem.

---

[60] Janusz Bugajski, "Trump's Criticisms Have Reinvigorated NATO," The Hill, February 7, 2019, https://thehill.com/opinion/national-security/428920-trumps-criticisms-have-reinvigorated-nato.

It is the way most people understand a problem. If a vendor no longer provides the high-quality product he did twenty-five years ago, a businessman knows to ask the vendor to up his game—or risk losing out on a lucrative contract. A bold, brash Queens businessman and your average heartland voter get this too. Contracts can be renegotiated, problems can be solved, and relationships can stay intact.

It reminds me of that old story about the boy who thought his father was a fool, and then as he grew up was surprised at how much his father had learned. Trump has been right all along; the media is just taking a while to catch up to what he is doing for this country.

NAFTA/USMCA

The intelligentsia has vacillated between mocking Trump for saying he would redo the North American Free Trade Agreement and ginning up false fears about the collapse of the economy and longstanding alliances if Trump dared to renegotiate it. But Trump rightly knows that alliances are only alliances if all parties are able to come to the table, a lesson one learns through hard-fought battles with labor unions, contractors, and politicians who both need business to happen and have their own motives for slowing down or speeding up a business deal. In boldly grasping anger over a twenty-five-year-old trade deal, Trump used the skills he learned as a real estate developer to say, "Why not? Why shouldn't our allies come to the table to renegotiate trade imbalances and negotiate on new issues that have developed in the past twenty-five years? Isn't that, after all, part of any good relationship, the ability to work through problems that arise for the greater purpose of holding the relationship together?" And thus it is that President Trump successfully negotiated the United States–Mexico–Canada Agreement (USMCA). It's common sense to Middle America voters that when something is going wrong, you can renegotiate. But to the foreign policy Establishment, renegotiating unfair alliances is not something taught in the halls of Georgetown's or Harvard's political science or government department. It is something you are prepared to do based on knowledge from hard-fought battles in New York's tough real estate market.

A popular phrase to describe someone's fortune is "right place, right time." But I feel this phrase undersells the reality of the situation. Good leaders, like Trump, *put themselves in the right place at the right time.*

The takeaway from this chapter should be clear: President Trump and Prime Minister Churchill both were prepared through their own experiences to boldly grasp the moment set in front of them.

4

FEARED AND DESPISED

The feckless and weak, who know they cannot lead, often try to stir up hatred against those who can, because they'd rather keep everyone down. It is the equal sharing of misery that lazy liberals support, since they do not want to spend the extra time to become good leaders themselves. That is why tenured professors and union-protected government employees do not like Trump; he may rock the boat by exposing the fraud that they perpetrate on the American people by preaching a gospel of laziness and mediocrity.

Trump and Churchill were both feared and despised coming into office. President Trump was hated by the media, leftist activists, think tanks, academics, and so on. But he also had to contend with being hated by some in the Republican Party, who wanted a more docile and amiable politician in office, whom they could get to do their bidding; think the Chamber of Commerce and Davos types who could hold their noses at a few pro-life or gun rights laws passed by the president, as long as corporate welfare and open borders were still allowed to flourish under a Republican president. Victor Davis Hanson describes the scenario as such: "Besides the Washington press and pundit corps, Donald Trump faced his third and more formidable opponent: the culture of permanent and senior employees of the federal and state governments, and the political appointees in Washington," who, as Hanson notes, are on a perpetual train that takes them from political appointments to jobs in the media, think tanks, academia, and so on, essentially waiting in the wings to trade one position for another, without much regard for the good of the country.[61]

Churchill also had to deal with entrenched interests and the intelligentsia, who doubted that he could successfully make important strategic decisions on issues both foreign and domestic. It is often forgotten in the annals of American history, often written by Marxists themselves who *know what happened* but *don't want others to know what happened*, that Stalin proposed at the 1943 Tehran conference a "wholesale, indiscriminate, mass execution of all German officers."[62] Churchill was the only one, it seems, who actually sharply criticized Stalin's suggestions, while the American delegation laughed them off. He was actually derided and despised for being willing to call out Stalin's probable violation of international law. He had the foresight to see "the loose language as an honest report from Stalin of just the kind of wanton brutality he would inflict upon any

[61] *The Case for Trump,* 179.
[62] Hourly History, *Winston Churchill: A Life from Beginning to* End (Amazon. com, 2017).

territory that fell under his domain."[63] Like Trump's prescient warnings about China and radical Islam, Churchill's warnings about Soviet aggression, which proved to be true, left Britain "criticized, derided, and accused of putting British colonial ambition ahead of the real war effort."[64]

Yes, colonial ambition or empire building is the old calling card of leftists who pretend they are opposing war but in reality are worried that their ideology will fall apart when confronted with Western civilization. Most leftists and opponents of Churchill weren't worried that he was going to stretch the United Kingdom too far or promote colonialism; they were worried that the Soviet Union, the one place they had finally convinced to practice communism, was going to fall at even the slightest push. Even worse, Churchill might expose the brutality and systematic human rights abuses occurring in the Soviet Union. They preferred the Potemkin villages; better to remain ignorant than possibly have your worldview blown up, after all.

It is easy to understand why Trump and Churchill were feared and despised. Consider the groups that most feared the election of Donald Trump:

▶ Academia: It's well understood that academia is a left-wing institution, fueled by billions of dollars in taxpayer funding, whether directly through public colleges or through federal financial aid, which has caused the cost of college to balloon. From an economic standpoint, there was no great reason to fear Trump's economic effect on college campuses vis-à-vis federal

---

[63] *A Life from Beginning to End.*
[64] *A Life from Beginning to End.*

funding; even some cuts would never close colleges. But what academia feared and despised the most about Trump was that he is not a liberal and he has given permission for conservative and right-leaning students on campus to speak out against political correctness. Imagine the pure horror on a gender studies professor's face if a student were to walk into class wearing a "Make America Great Again" hat.

▶ Radical Islamic terrorists: During the Obama administration, ISIS ran roughshod over one of the weakest and most ineffectual administrations in United States history (remember "Jobs for ISIS"? It was based on the argument that all that keeps radical terrorists from being upstanding citizens is a job, even though terrorists statistically come from educated, upper-middle-class families). Terrorists feared that Trump would decisively lead against ISIS in a way that would decimate them, which Trump actually did.

▶ The military-industrial complex: Oddly, liberals don't like how Trump has taken on the military-industrial complex, even though gray-haired sociology professors have been (sometimes rightly so) criticizing it for decades. As president, Trump negotiated with defense contractors on various contracts to bring down costs and save taxpayers money. It is true leadership like this that shows that Trump has the courage to take on the Establishment in all areas—even the defense industry, which tends to lean Republican. Trump is okay with losing potential donors and allies because he knows what he's doing is right.

The ISIS point deserves to be expanded on. In a 2017 article (meaning the numbers are probably even better now), Jamie McIntyre, a former Pentagon correspondent for CNN, writes:

> *The campaign liberated twice as many people and 18 percent more territory as in the previous 28 months under President Barack Obama, according to Defense Department figures. On Jan. 20—the day Trump was inaugurated—an estimated 35,000 ISIS fighters held approximately 17,500 square miles of territory in both Iraq and Syria. As of Dec. 21, the U.S. military estimates the remaining 1,000 or so fighters occupy roughly 1,900 squares miles of mostly barren desert primarily in Syria, where few people live, and where they will be forced to surrender or die. Between September 2014 when the counter-ISIS campaign began, and January 2017, U.S.-backed forces in Iraq and Syria liberated 13,200 square miles of territory and 2.4 million people from Islamic State rule. In the 11 months since Trump took office, an additional 15,570 square miles have been reclaimed and 5.3 million people have been liberated.*[65]

---

[65] Jamie McIntyre, "Here's How Much Ground ISIS Has Lost Since Trump Took Over," *Washington Examiner*, December 23, 2017, https://www.washingtonexaminer.com/heres-how-much-ground-isis-has-lost-since-trump-took-over.

And who opposed Churchill?

▶ Fascists. The website magazine *The National Interest* describes Churchill as "practically a lone voice in the 1930s against the danger of Hitlerism."[66]

▶ Communists.

▶ Weak European leaders.

Both men faced many enemies.

---

[66] Warfare History Network, "Hitler Nearly Took Over France's Battleship Fleet. Then Winston Churchill Stepped In," *The National Interest*, August 1, 2019, https://nationalinterest.org/blog/buzz/hitler-nearly-took-over-frances-battleship-fleet-then-winston-churchill-stepped-70496.

5

PATRIOTISM

"We have surmounted all the perils and endured all the agonies of the past. We shall provide against and thus prevail over the dangers and problems of the future, withhold no sacrifice, grudge no toil, seek no sordid gain, fear no foe. All will be well. We have, I believe, within us the life-strength and guiding light by which the tormented world around us may find the harbour of safety, after a storm-beaten voyage."[67]

—WINSTON CHURCHILL,
WRITING AT CHATEAU LAURIER, NOVEMBER 9, 1954

"Once more he was looking westward, convinced that the hope of England's security and, if it came to that, her deliverance lay across the Atlantic, in the vast untapped power of the United States. The fact that his mother had been American in no way diminished his loyalty to the Crown—he had been called 'fifty percent American and one hundred percent

[67] International Churchill Society, *Famous Quotes and Stories*, "No One Would Do Such Things," https://winstonchurchill.org/resources/quotes/famous-quotations-and-stories/.

British'—but he believed in bloodlines, was proud to have cousins across the sea."

—WILLIAM MANCHESTER, *THE LAST LION: WILLIAM SPENCER CHURCHILL—ALONE, 1932–1940*

"Each of you is graduating at a truly incredible time for our country. Our country is doing well. Our country is respected again. We are respected again. And we're reawakening American pride, American confidence, and American greatness. You know that. These gentlemen know it; I'll tell you right now. Thank you very much. Thank you very much. That's very nice. And we are restoring the fundamental principle that our first obligation and highest loyalty is to the American citizen. No longer will we sacrifice America's interests to any foreign power. We don't do that anymore. In all things and ways, we are putting America first, and it's about time."

—DONALD TRUMP,
U.S. AIR FORCE ACADEMY GRADUATION, 2019[68]

"For as long as heroes are written about, Winston Churchill will be written about. The proportions are all abundantly there. He was everything. The soldier who loved poetry. The historian who loved to paint. The diplomat who thrived on indiscretion. The patriot with international vision."

—WILLIAM F. BUCKLEY, *NATIONAL REVIEW*

Winston Churchill was a patriotic man, patriotic for England but also still having a love of the United States. And

---

[68] Donald J. Trump, "Remarks by President Trump at the 2019 United States Air Force Academy Graduation Ceremony, Colorado Springs, CO," whitehouse.gov, May 30, 2019, https://www.whitehouse.gov/briefings-statements/remarks-president-trump-2019-united-states-air-force-academy-graduation-ceremony-colorado-springs-co/.

despite what the fake news media tell you about Trump, Trump loves England too. A defender and lover of Western civilization will generally have fond thoughts and a place in his heart for England, which has done so much to advance Western civilization, in the same way the United States has advanced Western civilization and, arguably, English culture through the Bill of Rights and our system of laws.

Google "Donald Trump" and one of the first photos you are likely to see is of him hugging the American flag. The man loves America, but it's not just a superficial love of America; what motivates Trump is his patriotism, which to him means standing up for our veterans, our police officers, and the forgotten man. It also motivates his support for protecting free speech on campus, ending political correctness, and defeating the scourge of radical Islam. Like a mother bear protecting her cubs, Trump wants to protect American values because forces seek to threaten what he loves, which is America. Radical Islam seems to undermine core American values; leftist professors and triggered college students are seeking to destroy free speech on campus; and political correctness wants to force your daughter to shower in a locker room or use the bathroom next to a perverted old man who thinks he's a woman. It is patriotism that motivates President Trump to defend America from the enemies of Western civilization. It is also what Churchill spoke of when he argued for free speech and against political correctness, even without using that exact phrase.

Patriotism relies on two factors: love of country and honesty when your country needs to make improvements. But America as a whole is not flawed; rather, there are actors in our great country who seek to bring about harm to it. Trump stands up against harmful actors in his country, just like Churchill stood up against harmful actors in his country. Trump faces a larger problem in that social media and the internet have allowed haters of American greatness to make their views more widely known, more effectively and with greater efficiency. For example, groups like ISIS have used the internet to recruit vulnerable people into their ranks.[69]

In speaking on patriotism during a campaign speech, Churchill said, "Nothing is easier than to prevent free speech, but the only result of doing that is to reduce ourselves to those totalitarian States that were established by Hitler and Mussolini."[70] Andrew Roberts, in *Churchill: Walking with Destiny*, writes of "the courage and often lonely stands [Churchill] was to take against the twin totalitarian threats of Fascism and Communism.... [He] cared more for what he imagined would have been the good opinion of his fallen comrades of the Great War than for what was said by his living colleagues on the benches of the House of Commons."[71] Roberts could just as easily have been talking about political correctness or campus snowflakes. Likewise, Trump's patriotism is what led him to battle dictators in North Korea, Iran, and other countries. Hard-left journalists and the American haters in academia are flustered by how Trump could promise to rain down fire and fury on North Korea and then meet with Kim Jong-Un, but they

[69]   Antonia Ward, "ISIS's Use of Social Media Still Poses a Threat to Stability in the Middle East and Africa," The RAND Blog, December 11, 2018, https://www.rand.org/blog/2018/12/isiss-use-of-social-media-still-poses-a-threat-to-stability.html.
[70]   *Churchill: The Power of Words*, 362.
[71]   *Churchill: The Power of Words*, 2.

don't get what motivates Trump: the desire to protect America no matter what. Trump realizes in the sense of patriotism that he must do what is necessary to protect America; if military threats are not it, then diplomacy may be it. Protecting America is his goal, and like a good, strong leader, he is willing to change his mind and try new ideas to achieve his goal. Unlike liberals, he doesn't have blinders on and doesn't believe the means justify the ends.

Noting Churchill's patriotism, William Manchester writes, "The Empire! The mere mention of it aroused patriotic Britons like Churchill, made them brace their backs and lift their eyes. If there was any fixed star in their firmament it was an abiding faith in the everlasting glory of the realm."[72] Churchill was a man who loved his country.

In his campaign speeches Trump talked about, and he continues to talk about in the White House, the forgotten man and our great country. It is love of country. It is a hatred of seeing our brave men in uniform denigrated by anti-American Black Lives Matter radicals and the likes of Bill Ayers, who was either going to end up in a federal prison or academia (unfortunately for students he ended up in academia, but fortunately for prisoners he didn't end up in prison).

President Trump talked about this eloquently in his summer 2016 Republican National Convention speech, seeking to win over disaffected Democrats, Republicans, Independents, and the forgotten man. Remember that the world he was facing included a plethora of ills wrought by Barack Obama. Edward Klein, in his book *Guilty as Sin* about Hillary Clinton, lists:

---

[72] *Last Lion—Alone,* 44.

▶ "A feeble economy that fails to provide enough well-paying jobs to sustain a growing middle class."

▶ "Failing schools that do not prepare our children for the upheavals in technology, globalization, communications, medicine, and financial markets."

▶ "Unchecked immigration across our porous borders."

▶ "An increase in violent crime in most major American cities."

▶ "Runaway political correctness that prevents us from honestly talking about and solving our common problems."[73]

Now back to Trump's speech. He starts off by acknowledging the Republican Party but quickly pivots to "[W]e will lead our country back to safety, prosperity, and peace. We will be a country of generosity and warmth. But we will also be a country of law and order."

Our country. All of us—Democrat, Republican, Independent, black, white, gay, straight, and so on—will be led to the shared values of safety, peace, and prosperity[74] And although he offers a positive message to his audience, how we will make America great again, he also does not hide the truth from them or try to mislead them; he says, "Our Convention occurs at a moment of crisis for our nation. The attacks on our police, and the terrorism in our cities, threaten our very way of life.

[73] Edward Klein, *Guilty as Sin* (Washington, DC: Regnery Publishing, 2016), 238.

[74] "Full Text: Donald Trump 2016 RNC Draft Speech Transcript," Politico, July 21, 2016, https://www.politico.com/story/2016/07/full-transcript-donald-trump-nomination-acceptance-speech-at-rnc-225974.

Any politician who does not grasp this danger is not fit to lead our country." Hillary Clinton, obviously the target of his criticism, did not grasp the danger of radical Islam, because the echo chamber of the Council on Foreign Relations and Sidney Blumenthal told her to focus on other issues. And neither did Obama, who was one of the worst foreign policy leaders this country has ever seen, and that includes in his own party, which includes the racist Woodrow Wilson and the naïve FDR (just read the parts about Churchill in this book to see how bad a leader FDR was when it came to seeing the threats posed by Stalin and Hitler).

Despite being labeled as arrogant or egotistical, Trump actually is incredibly humble in this speech; he acknowledges that the police and our military would help solve these problems. He could lead, as a presidential speech should of course argue, but he alone could not solve the problems facing the country.

And here's where you can't trust the fake news media: he said the phrase "I alone" only once, and it was not to talk about all the political issues or all the issues facing the country; it was specifically to talk about the problem of a rigged political system, because he himself was familiar with that system, having had to play the New York political real estate game for so many years (and he played it incredibly well). That is what is important to note. President Trump recognizes his limitations and wants better for the country. Churchill and Trump recognize and appreciate patriotism. Churchill fought valiantly for the country he loved, and Trump fights valiantly against the following:

▶ *The DNC*

▶ *Republicans in Name Only (RINOS)*

▶ *The FBI*

▶ *The DOJ*

▶ *The media*

▶ *Barack Obama*

▶ *Hillary Clinton*

▶ *James Comey*

▶ *Andrew McCabe*

▶ *Robert Mueller*

▶ *Rod Rosenstein*

▶ *Mitt Romney*

▶ *Russia*

▶ *China*

▶ *North Korea*

▶ *Syria*

▶ *Iran*

▶ *ISIS*

▶ *Illegal immigrants*

▶ *Twitter warriors*

He fights them for the country he loves and the people he loves: police officers, veterans, business owners, union members, religious people, and anyone else who wants a better life.

In another situation, Prime Minister Churchill had to make an "England First" decision, and one that exemplified the patriotism of putting your country first, which can be considered true nationalism, because it protects the rights and prosperity of everyone in a country, in opposition to racist ethnonationalism, which seeks to help only one race or ethnicity.

One of Churchill's most patriotic decisions may have been one of the most controversial he ever made. But in making the right decision in the short term for England, Churchill ultimately sent the right message that allowed the Allied forces to win World War II.

In 1940, France was doing what it does best: surrendering, in this case to Germany. This involved the clear possibility that Germany would be able to acquire France's large navy. According to the International Churchill Society, "With these ships in his hands, Hitler's threat to invade Britain could become a reality. Churchill had to make a choice. He could either trust the promises of the new French government that they would never hand over their ships to Hitler. Or he could make sure that the ships never joined the German navy by destroying them himself."[75]

And that is exactly what Churchill did in the infamous Attack on Mers-el-Kébir. PBS describes the attack thusly:

> Churchill took matters into his own hands. He launched Operation Catapult to capture the French Fleet before it returned to French waters. A number of the most powerful French battleships were docked at a naval base in the French-Algiers port of Mers-el-Kébir. Churchill issued the French an ultimatum: Give up the vessels to the British, sail them to Allied ports, or face attack from the Royal Navy.

---

[75] International Churchill Society, "Churchill's Deadly Decision: Destroying the French Fleet," https://winstonchurchill.org/resources/in-the-media/churchill-in-the-news/destroying-the-french-fleet/.

The French stalled, hoping for the arrival of reinforcements. The deadline passed, and the British attacked with devastating force, destroying a number of French ships and killing 1,300 French sailors—more than the number of French soldiers killed by the Germans at that point in the war.

France declared the action a horrific act of mass murder. Germany used it to release anti-Britain propaganda in Europe. Britain stood firmly by its leader and supported Churchill's decision. But most importantly, Roosevelt saw the attack as a confirmation of British resolve, and soon supplied Britain with the 50 destroyers it so desperately needed.[76]

And now here is what Churchill himself said of the decision the next day, in front of the House of Commons. In his speech, Churchill makes clear he knows that he may be despised for his decision but explains why what he did was right and was the final viable option:

Thus I must place on record that what might have been a mortal injury was done to us by the Bordeaux Government with full known knowledge of the consequences and of our dangers, and after rejecting all our appeals at the moment when they were abandoning the Alliance, and breaking the engagements which fortified it.... I leave the judgment of our action, with confidence, to Parliament. I leave it to the nation, and I leave it to the United States. I leave it to the world and to history.[77]

---

[76] "Churchill's Deadly Decision: Preview," *Secrets of the Dead: Unearthing History*, April 16, 2010, pbs.org, https://www.pbs.org/wnet/secrets/churchills-deadly-decision-preview-this-episode/548/.

[77] *Churchill: The Power of Words*, 253–258.

Historians will absolutely question Churchill's decision for years, but let me make a firm judgment about what Churchill did: he showed the enemy that he would make tough decisions to save his country and to protect the greater interests of Western civilization. Would other leaders have been able to make the decision? Likely not, except for President Trump. Many left-wing historians forget that they have twenty-twenty hindsight and so are always ready to judge past decisions by present-day values (the only time hard leftists apply values in their life), a fact worth remembering when reading their historical "analyses."

As stated earlier in this book, in all my life I never thought I would see a leader who was as great a defender of Western civilization and Western values as Winston Churchill. Then Donald Trump came along, and I became convinced that he could equal and possibly surpass Churchill.

A true leader is able to make the tough choices and is able to put what is right in front of optics. A good leader does what is best for his country, even if his harshest critics will write columns or tweets criticizing the decision.

6

PRESCIENCE

In order to be a defender of Western civilization, one must have prescience. One cannot always act against what one sees coming on the horizon right away; one must sometimes try to use one's words or actions to prod those in the best position at the time to act on it. For example, President Trump rightly saw looming trade issues, like with China, and foreign policy issues, like with ISIS. He could do only so much as a private citizen, but he still went on *Fox & Friends* regularly to voice his opinion, knowing that key politicians and consultants watched the show. He would have loved it if President Obama had taken decisive action against China or destroyed ISIS or at least called out radical Islam for what it really was. But Obama did not do that. Understandably then, private citizen Donald Trump tried to influence a potential future president, who turned out to be a weak, low-energy loser, by endorsing him in the 2012 presidential race. Even if he wasn't a huge fan of Romney, Trump could place a bet that he, if elected, would be his best bet.

Churchill, too, took bold gambles, particularly with his prescience regarding the threat of the Soviet Union. He was the only major Allied leader to strongly warn of the threats from Stalin; had people listened to him sooner, we could have avoided a lot of issues (for example, the Cold War). It wouldn't have been hard for Truman to take more decisive action, for example. He, after all, invited Churchill to speak in Missouri, where Churchill warned, "A shadow has fallen upon the scenes so lately lighted by the Allied victory." And though he acknowledged that "nobody knew what Soviet Russia" specifically intended to do, Churchill still warned famously that "an iron curtain has descended across the Continent."[78]

The International Churchill Society sums up the reaction to his speech:

> *Simple truths stated or not, the outcry was immediate. Stalin of course reacted "with grim evidence of his paranoia," Margaret Truman noted in her biography of her father. "He accused the United States of allying itself with Great Britain to thwart Russia. He declared Churchill's speech at Fulton was an unfriendly act. 'Such a speech if directed against the United States would never have been permitted in Russia.' Never was there more tragic evidence of the Russian dictator's complete inability to understand a free society." But there also was critical reaction in the West, the United States and Britain included. Among other American critics, Senator Claude Pepper (D-FL) not only denounced the speech but warned against becoming "a guarantor of British imperialism." James*

---

[78] *Churchill: The Power of Words*, 370.

Roosevelt, son of the late president, said Winston's statement at Fulton represented only "the British point of view."[79]

In writing as well, Churchill warned of the threat of the Soviet Union as early as the 1920s but still expressed optimism. In one memorable article, Churchill wrote:

When all was over, Torture and Cannibalism were the only two expedients that the civilized, scientific Christian States had been able to deny themselves; and these were of doubtful utility. But nothing daunted the valiant heart of man. Son of the Stone Age, vanquisher of nature with all her trials and monsters, he met the awful and self-inflicted agony with new reserves of fortitude. Freed in the main by his intelligence from mediaeval fears, he marched to death with sombre dignity.... Moreover, we have emerged victoriously and safely from the appalling conflict in which so many powerful states were dashed to pieces, and the British Empire, united, extended, erect, occupies at this moment a leading place among the Governments of men and the most glorious pinnacle ever reached in all of our history.[80]

William Manchester notes that Churchill had reasons to be bitter for the way England made him a scapegoat. But when it came time to confront Nazi Germany, Churchill was the man for the job. Manchester writes of the appeasers in the British government who thought they were right and that the Germans would play nice if England let them do what they wanted.

---

[79]   C. Brian Kelly, Excerpt: "Best Little Stories from the Life and Times of Winston Churchill," International Churchill Society, https://winstonchurchill.org/publications/churchill-bulletin/bulletin-033-mar-2011/excerpt-best-little-stories-from-the-life-and-times-of-winston-churchill/.

[80]   *Churchill: The Power of Words*, 156.

Summing up how Churchill was ultimately recognized as the right one to save them, Manchester concludes the second volume of this three-volume series on Churchill by writing this:

> So, with their [the appeasers'] eyes open, they sought accommodation with a criminal regime, turned a blind eye to its iniquities, ignored its frequent resort to murder and torture, submitted to extortion, humiliation, and abuse, until, having sold out to all who had sought to stand shoulder to shoulder with Britain and keep the bridge against the new barbarism, they led England herself into the cold damp shadow of the gallows, friendless save for the demoralized republic across the channel.

Pause here for a minute. Manchester is savaging the English people for giving in so easily to the Germans and then, in an act of poetic justice, turning back to Churchill to save them in their time of trouble. Although it's probably safe to say that Churchill had a bit of an "I told you so" moment, he did accept their apologies by recognition. Manchester concludes:

> Their end came when the House of Commons, in a revolt of conscience, wrenched power from them and summoned to the colors the one man who had foretold all that had passed.... [W]ith the reins of power at last firm in his grasp, he resolved to lead Britain and her fading empire in one last great struggle worthy of all they had been and meant, to arm the nation, not only with weapons but also with the mace of honor, creating in every English breast a soul beneath the ribs of death.[81]

---

[81] *Last Lion— Alone*, 689.

A soul beneath the ribs of death? What Manchester is saying is that Churchill breathed new life into his people and restored to them hope—hope that Nazi Germany could be defeated and Western civilization would be saved.

And looking back, in one of his final speeches, Churchill sums up what he had predicted, what he had seen, and what he viewed as lying ahead:

> *The question we may ask ourselves is how the balance lies between progress and ruin. When we contemplate the squalid and brutal destruction of the last war, man's ingenuity in perfecting the means of his own annihilation, and the jealousy, anxiety, and hatred that consume a large part of the globe, it is easy to give a melancholy answer.... Yet amidst this somber and perplexing scene there is much that is bright. With all our political differences we in this country are, I think, more united than we have ever been in time of peace. Certainly we may disagree, but I see no hatred. The way ahead is a broad and clear one.*[82]

As discussed in Chapter 3, a good leader may spend his whole life preparing, not knowing the exact challenge he will be taking on but preparing to have the courage to take on any issues. Again, President Trump had the prescience to see problems, speak of them, and wait to see if anyone else acted before he finally decided that he had to run for president if he wanted to see a fix made. But prescience involves not only seeing a problem but also knowing how to message regarding the problem, in order to become that leader. Plenty of people have great ideas; Trump has the ability to communicate his views and leadership

---

[82] *Churchill: The Power of Words*, 428.

on those issues. As discussed in the chapter on genius, Trump can boil down key ideas into easy-to-understand ones. Part of Trump's prescience, which sets him up to be the defender of Western civilization, is the way he knows how to get attuned to the needs and thoughts of Middle America. He had a successful show on NBC, a liberal network; he regularly called in to Fox News, a conservative network; he kept up a political presence in Florida, which he knew was integral to any presidential bid; and he was a regular guest and friend to people such as Howard Stern, a famous shock jock who knows how to talk to the average person. Like a good intelligence officer, Trump has found a way to keep his pulse on the whole country, by interacting with a variety of media. Of course, Trump's favorite newspaper is his hometown *New York Times*. Undoubtedly, Trump's daily reading of the *New York Times* allows him to see issues developing on the horizon, while also seeing the disconnect in how various groups—conservatives, liberals, independents, business owners, and so forth—discuss an issue.

It is actually Trump's prescience that scares liberals. They see Trump's ability to see a situation unfolding and to make a strong decision, which puts them in a trap. This is a skill Trump had to learn as a real estate developer: being able to figure out what areas would be popular in ten, fifteen, or thirty years and then making investments to reap rewards down the road.

For example, as I write this, the left is now in a tizzy over Trump's decision to enforce the public-charge rule in immigration law, which gives the U.S. the right to deny green cards to immigrants who are likely to be a burden on taxpayers. All along, leftists have been saying that all immigrants, including illegal immigrants, contribute economically to this country.

Now they are saying that barring immigrants from receiving welfare if they want to obtain a green card is a form of discrimination, thus forcing them to defend the idea of immigrants' receiving welfare, thus reinforcing conservative arguments against unlimited, unchecked immigration.

And like Churchill, Trump has seen people come back to him after supporting appeasement. For example, right now there are serious discussions about the ways Iran is (shock) violating the Iranian nuclear agreement. But when Obama, most likely illegally, pushed it through, many people, and even some Republicans, praised him for appeasing the Iranian dictatorship. And then again, when Trump moved to undo the agreement, he was criticized. Yet, leading intelligence experts and defense experts agree that the Iranians are breaking the deal and that Trump is right. Of course, what's best about this is that it's not exactly shocking to anyone with any sense that the Iranians would break this deal. After all, Iran has one of the worst human rights records, including its oppressing women and homosexuals. But what was important to failed presidential candidate John Kerry and failed president Barack Obama was that they have something they could point to as a foreign policy achievement after Libya collapsed under Obama and Clinton, and after our allies distrusted us after Obama backtracked and failed to lead from the front. As Churchill did, Trump has been able to forge ahead and begin to protect American interests in a way President Obama failed to do.

Prescience is a great skill, and Trump and Churchill both used it to defend Western civilization. They defended the Western civilization values of protecting human rights and standing up against totalitarian forces, whether those forces be fascism or Islamic totalitarianism. For Trump and Churchill, whether or not history ultimately judges them as great leaders does not matter as much to them as having done the right thing and protecting Western civilization from its enemies. This leads us into the next chapter, on instinct, in which I will continue to talk about the roles that experience and knowledge have in the decision-making and leadership process.

7

INSTINCT

In this chapter, I'll explore the role of instinct in the ways that Prime Minister Churchill and President Trump defended Western civilization. Primarily they did this through acquiring knowledge throughout their lives and then knowing how to apply it. An analogy would be how athletes develop muscle memory; it might be awkward and there will be mistakes at first, but with practice, a good wide receiver develops the instinct to know exactly when to turn to make a catch, or a hockey goalie knows exactly where the puck is going, because his body has been trained so many times that he has mentally and physically absorbed the necessary skill.

Similarly, Churchill and Trump developed instinct or a gut feeling throughout their years in private and public life. I have touched on many of these experiences throughout this book, but I want to reiterate a few key moments to set the stage for this chapter.

Trump knows how to talk politics because he was previously involved on the edges of politics his whole life, as is necessitated by being a New York real estate developer. But in addition to what we may view as traditional politics, such as schmoozing politicians, donating to the right people, and articulating a vision, he also learned the art of the deal and the art of understanding people through his time in New York real estate (I talked about this in the chapter on genius). Instinct is not something you are born with—it is something that is developed throughout your life. A good leader takes in information, absorbs it, makes a decision, then takes feedback and recalibrates. A great example is how Trump watches television and uses this to influence how he talks about an issue. Although often criticized for the way he watches shows like *Fox & Friends*, this is actually a great strategy. Remember, Trump doesn't need to watch Fox News to learn about foreign policy, as he can call any ambassador, any CEO, any military leader in the world to learn what is going on in any place. But what he learns from shows like *Fox & Friends* is how to talk about an issue in a way that the average American who may have only an hour or so to watch the news can digest. In this way, Trump has developed an instinct for communicating to the American people, which clearly has served him well, judging from his steady, if not rising, approval ratings and of course his upset victory in 2016.

Trump is able to use this ability to understand the average American to defend Western civilization by understanding how most Americans are talking about an issue. Let's take the example of tariffs. Most Americans, especially Republicans, generally support the ideas of free enterprise and entrepreneurship. The values of Western civilization, as described previously, include limited taxation and free markets. That being said, Trump has recognized that some people might have become so disillusioned by the negative effects of trade deals such as NAFTA or the Dominican Republic–Central America Free Trade Agreement (CAFTA), and the proposed Trans-Pacific Partnership, that they would turn against free enterprise and embrace a Socialist candidate such as Bernie Sanders and Socialist policies in general (the seemingly shared position on trade by Sanders and Trump has often been pointed out by Trump's critics on the right).

But what Trump has done is say he supports free trade (and by extension free enterprise), but that what countries like China are engaging in is an example of unfair trade and has actually harmed capitalism and free markets. In other words, he has acknowledged that tariffs are not ideal but has framed the issue in such a way as to make it clear that tariffs might be the best option at the moment, thereby showing voters he understands their concerns while also supporting the principles of free enterprise. In this way, Trump has been relatively successful in balancing his concerns about trade with his overall support for free enterprise and commerce. For this reason, the markets often initially get jittery when Trump talks about tariffs, but then most financial advisers and traders see that he is using this talk to enter into negotiations with countries like China, and then most people understand that he is using it as leverage to seek a fair trading system that balances business interests and benefits against the very real losses some people face from trade.

In terms of these instincts, Trump very much echoes Prime Minister Churchill, who accumulated a wide array of knowledge and experience throughout his political career, taking some victories with losses, as many Churchill historians have noted.

Biographer Roy Jenkins opens his book *Churchill* with this description: "Churchill was far too many faceted, idiosyncratic and unpredictable a character to allow himself to be imprisoned by the circumstances of his birth. His devotion to his career and his conviction that he was a man of destiny were far stronger than any class or tribal loyalty."[83]

Growing up, Churchill began to develop the ability to persevere through hard times and build the instincts to get through tough times. Jenkins continues with his description of Churchill's life, by pointing out:

▶ Churchill was born premature into a family stuck in debt by a poor financial deal.

▶ It's been debated, but there is a possibility that Churchill and his brother were half-brothers, implying infidelity in his family.

▶ His father was ill for many years, including his last three years.

▶ This led to a series of different men and fathers in Churchill's life.[84]

In fact, Jenkins was so impressed with the way Churchill persevered that he ends his almost one-thousand-page book with this comment about Churchill and another prime minister, William Gladstone: "When I started writing this book I thought that Gladstone was, by a narrow margin, the greater man, certainly the more remarkable specimen of humanity.

---

[83] Roy Jenkins, *Churchill: A Biography* (New York: Plume Publishing, 2001), 1.
[84] Jenkins, 18.

In the course of writing it I have changed my mind. I now put Churchill, with all his idiosyncrasies, his indulgences, his occasional childishness, but also his genius, his tenacity and his persistent ability, right or wrong, successful or unsuccessful, to be larger than life, as the greatest human being ever to occupy 10 Downing Street."[85]

Throughout this book, I discuss different times of trial in Winston Churchill's life, so I will not cover too many right now, but suffice it to say that Churchill faced difficult circumstances and situations throughout his life. It is these circumstances that we can assume allowed Churchill to become a defender of Western civilization, saving England, Europe, and the world as a whole from fascism and the Soviet Union, making up for any prior mistakes he had made throughout his career in politics. He developed the ability to defend the ideals of Western civilization, such as free enterprise, free speech, and respect for human rights for all people.

Instinct, again, is not something you are born with, but rather something that is developed. Both Trump and Churchill were great at developing their instincts, and because of that skill and of the work of both these men, Western civilization and everything it entails still stand proud today.

---

[85] Jenkins, 912.

8

DEFIANCE

Everyone was against him. The Bush family, with their deep financial network and political network. Ted Cruz and Marco Rubio, with their grassroots energy. The young libertarian students ready to knock on doors and make phone calls all day for Rand Paul. Other candidates also had a deeper donor list from hard-fought election battles, as in the case of Scott Walker, or from years in public office, as in the case of Rick Perry. But Trump defied the conventional wisdom to defeat them during the primary race, notwithstanding the toughest network of all: the Clintons and their pals in Wall Street finance and in the levers of government. He defeated them all to take his rightful role as a defender of Western civilization. And while we're at it, it's worth mentioning that the chief cheerleader of the Never Trump movement, that favorite movement of the Council on Foreign Relations, pro-amnesty, and illegal immigrants crowd, *The Weekly Standard*, went bankrupt, which unfortunately has not shut up Bill Kristol, who is still a favorite of the anti-Trump left and those diehards in the Republican Party (a very small number, since 94 percent of Republicans approve of Trump and/or plan to vote for him in 2020).

Churchill too had to defy his critics and conventional foreign policy wisdom to become the twentieth-century defender of Western civilization.

Defiance is the ability to persevere when times get tough, but also describes when someone overcomes challenges or challenges norms, defying conventional standards. Both Churchill and Trump defied the traditional political norms of their time to rise to the top.

President Trump defiantly became president by breaking social norms and basically doing everything you're not supposed to do if you're running for office. First, let's start with his political background. He considered several runs for president, but at the end of the day, when he announced he was running for president, he had yet to hold any elected office, nor had he been a judge or been appointed an ambassador or anything like that. He had never run a government agency. In other words, his political experience was unorthodox not just for becoming president but for running even for the U.S. Senate or House.

Second, the way he campaigned defied social norms, allowing him to take his case for how he would defend Western civilization right to the people, and in a way that would garner media coverage (five billion dollars' worth of free media coverage after all). It's this point I'll now turn to.

Trump's presidential campaign was obviously successful, but also unconventional, which made it successful. An interesting part of Trump's defiance of convention that has been overlooked in most discussions is the way Trump dressed during rallies, always in a suit. Conventional wisdom from the

Beltway consultant class would be to try to come off as one of the people by wearing blue jeans and a white shirt, no tie, collar open, for a rally. Not Trump. He wore a suit to every rally and almost always had his signature ties on (part of the Trump Signature Collection). To many, this would seem to make no sense; if you're trying to appeal to disaffected voters and people in Middle America, wouldn't you try to dress like a working guy? Trump was a New York billionaire who owned multiple country clubs and golf courses. And people understood this and appreciated how he was genuine in a way that politician-in-a-box Mitt Romney was not. By defying convention, Trump connected better with people because he was forthright about who he was, even oftentimes bringing up how rich he was.

Finally, the way Trump talked about the issues showed defiance, because he talked about the issues the way he wanted to talk about them, definitively, 100 percent, not the way a high-paid consultant would tell him to talk about the issues. In doing this, he rejected the Beltway, swamp polling firms, and consultant class and talked freely about issues.

I've talked about this throughout the book, but in this chapter I want to return to the way Trump speaks and discuss more specifically how that is an act of defiance. He is not just defying norms but defying his enemies who do not want him to speak the way he does (because they knew his style is successful and that if he changed, he would lose).

▶ **Immigration:** Trump did not say that Mexican immigrants or all immigrants were criminals and rapists. He said some rapists were coming over through illegal immigration. He also did not call immigrants "animals," he said that of MS-13, a gang that brutally kills people, rapes young girls, and terrorizes communities *including and most of all Hispanic communities*. They are animals for the ways they treat human beings; one of the MS-13 members actually went by the name Animal. Trump was not afraid to call out the crimes of violent illegal immigrants, such as the animal who killed Kate Steinle. This is something Jeb Bush, the Bush family, and the Chamber of Commerce types are afraid to do; after all, Jeb Bush called illegal immigration an act of love. Trump also defied standards by laying out a clear plan: build the wall; deport violent, criminal illegal immigrants; and then maybe we talk about what to do with everyone else.

▶ **Abortion:** Trump was the first presidential candidate that we know of to so clearly call out the Democrats for their extreme stance on abortion, when he said, during a presidential debate, that Hillary Clinton supported abortion up until the moment of birth, which is, in fact, the platform of the Democratic Party. He later expanded on this, after the governor of Virginia, Ralph Northam, came out in support of infanticide, leading Trump to repeatedly say that the governor of Virginia endorsed the execution of babies, which is actually what Northam did support.

▶ **Outreach to African Americans:** In a memorable speech, candidate Donald Trump noted how the schools in heavily minority areas were failing, how jobs were scarce, and how crime was out of control. He ended with a simple question: What do you have to lose by voting Republican once? Of course the Democrats got so mad at this they leaped out of their white enclaves in the Hamptons or Martha's Vineyard and immediately found a TV station on which to denounce Trump, because they realized Trump was defying the unspoken rule of politics: don't say that heavily African American cities have been decimated by decades of the big-government, high-tax, anti-cop politics of the Democratic Party. Even now, as I write this book, there is a controversy because Trump has called out Congressman Elijah Cummings for having a district in Baltimore overrun with rats and ruined by high unemployment, forcing Cummings and other officials in the area to say that Cummings has done quite well as a leader but also Trump needs to give them billions in taxpayer dollars to fix poverty. (Which is it?)

Defiance requires the ability to fight. Churchill showed defiance throughout his life by overcoming adversity as a child and overcoming hatred among his own people, and even among his own party. Trump defied convention to become president. This defiance is strongly linked to each's pugnacity, the focus of the next chapter.

9

PUGNACITY

One of the arguments from hard-core Trump supporters is
that he fights. And this in fact is something to praise him
for. When we envision a defender of Western civilization, we
want someone with pugnacity, someone who can stare down
North Korean dictators, German leaders who sacrifice their
own country at the altar of the refugees, and trade cheaters like
China. At heart, a defender must be a fighter; you don't need a
defender unless you're in a fight.

In contrast to his 2016 presidential opponent, who said "I'm
with her," Trump made it clear in his 2016 Republican National
Convention speech that he didn't want people to fight for him.
He wanted to fight for them. In his speech, Trump noted that
his slogan would be, "I'm with you." But it's not just as president
that Trump is fighting, of course. He fought through a bankruptcy that almost ruined his life (a story about Trump has him
looking at a homeless person and musing that the homeless
person has a higher net worth than he did at the time). He fought
through the tabloids, through the mainstream media, through

seventeen worthy presidential primary opponents. And now he is fighting for us—against the establishment, against the deep state, against the fake news media. It is Trump's pugnacity that makes him the greatest defender of Western civilization the world will ever see.

Victor Davis Hanson notes that our best leaders, at the right time, and as noted above, boldly grasping a notice, can often be fighters and rough around the edges: "Trump's cunning and mercurialness—honed in Manhattan real estate, global sales-manship, reality TV, and wheeler-dealer investments—may have earned him ostracism from polite Washington society." And yet, this was not a flaw for Trump and for the time; his pugnacity benefitted the United States. "But these talents also may for a time be suited to dealing with many of the outlaws of the global frontier, such as the Iranian theocracy or North Korea's Kim Jong-un." In other words, Trump's pugnacity is right for the time and right for the challenges. When someone is being picked on or being bullied or taken advantage of, as the United States was under Obama's weak leadership, when he basically let other countries write our environmental and nuclear laws, people were prepared to put up with someone a bit rough around the edges, a bit unconventional in terms of background. Financial radio host Dave Ramsey often gives the advice to people considering divorce or going through a messy divorce that they should hire an attorney whom they find off-putting or distasteful; similarly, a classic tactic in the old days of corporate takeovers was to find a mean and rude attorney to represent you, because you wanted someone who was going to play hardball.

Through his career, Churchill too showed pugnacity, being willing to fight for what he knew was right, and making tough decisions. Western civilization and those who have protected its values rely on someone who is willing to fight and even be rough around the edges when necessary to protect those values. Churchill developed this ability through actual fighting early in his life. As a correspondent and recently out of the military at age twenty-four, Churchill found himself on a train attacked by Boers while he was covering the Anglo-Boer War (the second one). He describes the experience this way:

"I found myself alone in a shallow cutting and none of our soldiers who had all surrendered on the way, to be seen. Then suddenly there appeared on the line at the end of the cutting two men not in uniform"—men whom Churchill recognizes as Boers. He continues, "Two bullets passed, both within a foot, one on either side.... I knew nothing of white flags, and the bullets had made me savage."[86] Though Churchill escaped alive by surrendering (because he didn't have his gun on him), it still shows how he fought, by figuring out a way to stay alive and to initially escape them, surrendering after the soldiers, who were presumably armed, did. This only began his journey, where he spent almost four weeks in a prisoner-of-war camp, escaping and eventually finding shelter in a coal mine and then returning home, where "I found that during the weeks I had been a prisoner of war my name had resounded at home.... The British nation was smarting under a series of military reverses such as are so often necessary to evoke the exercise of its strength, and

---

[86] *Churchill: The Power of Words*, 29.

the news of my outwitting the Boers was received with enormous and no doubt disproportionate satisfaction."[87]

Hmm. During a war England was fighting in, the people were demoralized and thought they might surely lose. Then, Churchill was able to inspire hope in them that they would win and defeat evil. It seems this incident was setting Churchill up for his leadership role during World War II by teaching him about morale and how to literally rally the troops.

---

[87] *Churchill: The Power of Words*, 36.

10

EBULLIENCE

In this final chapter, I'll talk about the role of ebullience in being a defender of Western civilization. Being ebullient means being cheerful and full of energy, or can be thought of as being full of joy. Churchill and Trump both approached their work with a sense of joy and energy. When defending a civilization from external threats, it is vital that the leader does not let himself get down but instead exudes energy, a love of country, and a love of values.

Writing about Churchill, Frances James says:

> There is nothing passive about Peace, in either the seeking or possession of it. Its quest demands eternal vigilance, positive thought. Its possession demands resolute preparedness to defend it. He who would disturb the peace never sleeps. Nor does the man of peace passively await his assaults. If you want peace, you must defend it, seek out the disturber, detect him from afar, nail him down, vanquish him.
>
> The ebullience of youth understood, there was no inconsistency between Churchill's devotion to peace and his first

profession of arms. That purpose soon became manifest in the subordination of sword to pen, which marked his long life. The first halting, painful speech in the Mother of Parliaments, at the turn of the century, did more than show the spirit which overcame defects of voice and vision: it revealed the mind to which "patriotism" meant peace, and the defence of the realm, never war or wanton aggression.

What he did for more than half a century thereafter was almost uniquely significant; how he did it is something people will discuss for ever; why he did it is of transcendent importance to us all.... When we speak of him to our children, let us speak of them, too; without malice, with firmness and measured magnanimity, as he did. But let us not forget them and what they stand for, lest we spurn his bequest to us, betray all he stood for, and drop the vital lessons of history in the rubbish bin.

To praise God for his life and example, to cherish and revere his memory, is not alone enough: it is empty, unless we see clearly what we praise and revere in truth, and unless the same prophetic spirit and action prevail in our children's lives forever.[88]

When people speak of Churchill, they talk of the joy he t in his work. It can be easy to get beat up and beat yourself when you have the weight of the world on your shoulders, Churchill took it in stride and with great joy.

I want to unpack that excellent writing by Frances Jai and explore a bit more how it shows Churchill's ebullient nat

---

[88] Frances James, "The Fire of Life—Churchill as Personality of the C tury: Finest Hour 100, Autumn 1998," International Churchill Soc https://winstonchurchill.org/publications/finest-hour/finest-hour-1 the-fire-of-life-churchill-as-personality-of-the-century/.

Being a political leader can be tough, and being a political leader during times of war when there are countries all over fighting one another is even tougher. James says it well: "There is nothing passive about Peace, in either the seeking or possession of it. Its quest demands eternal vigilance, positive thought. Its possession demands resolute preparedness to defend it." In other words, you have to always be prepared and always be preparing in order to seek peace and to keep Western civilization alive in the face of its enemies. But in doing so, you cannot always be angry; you must remain ebullient, maintaining a joy to drive you. Put another way: do not get upset or overwhelmed by the task in front of you; rather, like a parent raising a child, thank God and be joyful that you've been given this opportunity, this sacred honor to lead and to protect what is important for generations to come. You must remain ebullient, joyful, optimistic, because what you are doing is working to protect what is so important and what must be guarded every single day.

In the next part, James writes, "When we speak of him to our children, let us speak of them, too; without malice, with firmness and measured magnanimity, as he did. But let us not forget them and what they stand for, lest we spurn his bequest to us, betray all he stood for, and drop the vital lessons of history in the rubbish bin." In this, James is reflecting the way Churchill would have wanted people to speak of him. People should not disparage Churchill for mistakes he shouldn't have made. Acknowledge them but remember that what he did ultimately worked out for England and so he made the right decisions.

Finally, James writes, "To praise God for his life and example, to cherish and revere his memory, is not alone enough: it is empty, unless we see clearly what we praise and revere in truth,

and unless the same prophetic spirit and action prevail in our children's lives forever." Here, he is arguing that we cannot just say, "Churchill was a great guy." Rather, we must understand what happened, understand the truth of the situation, and work so that future generations understand what Churchill did in order to protect England, Europe, and the rest of the world from near-certain destruction.

In this way, I do once again see a strong similarity between Prime Minister Churchill and President Trump. Citizens today will have to raise the next generation to understand what Trump has done and help them put his actions and words into context, because he too is often misunderstood, often because the mainstream media work overtime to try to discredit him. It's to Trump's legacy and his work that we now turn.

It is with this great joy and love of country that Trump approaches all his work, whether as a builder, checking in on every project and talking to every worker, or as a president, regularly traveling to the heartland and to the forgotten people to share with them the joy of making America great again.

Trump's ebullience plays into his role as a communicator and how he defends Western civilization by giving people great joy. To see Trump at a campaign stop is not to watch an ordinary politician give a stump speech. His campaign events at times have simply included his reading the paper and commenting on stories he sees. They don't feel as much like political events as like Trump and tens of thousands of his closest friends gathering together to talk politics and share about their lives. Despite the media caricature of Trump and his supporters as being angry or bitter, they are in fact full of love and full of joy. Watching his rallies, we see a blend of veterans, fathers, mothers, millennials, people of all races and religions united around one cause: making America great again. Considering that many of Trump's supporters are naturally suspicious and wary of classic political talk, it is amazing, and a sign of Trump's ebullience, that they come hours early and listen to an hour-and-a-half or two-hour-long speech without there ever being a feeling of a loss of energy in the room.

In fact, some of the most passionate supporters of Trump are minorities, including gay people like Scott Pressler, or African Americans like Lynnette Hardaway and Rochelle Richardson, popularly known as Diamond and Silk. In defending Western civilization, Trump has been able to pull together a true rainbow coalition of people united around issues like reducing crime in our inner cities, providing economic opportunities, and destroying radical Islam. Trump not only exudes ebullience but also inspires it. He gives people hope and joy that it will be morning in America. That they will be given an opportunity to realize the American dream. That he will do the most a politician can do to create optimism and create opportunity for everyone.

Of course, this contrasts sharply with what his leftist critics say. They frequently use terms like "hatemonger," "fearmonger," "racist," or "nativist" to turn people against Trump, because they see how he is effective. The greatest fear for leftists is not that Trump will divide Americans; it's that he will unite them. And by and large, Trump has united Americans with his ebullience. He was able to get LGBT Americans, who had concerns about gay marriage or transgender bathrooms, to unite with conservative Christians against the common enemy of radical Islam, after the Pulse nightclub shooting. Being protected from terrorism is a uniting factor, not a dividing issue, like whether Christian bakers should be forced to bake wedding cakes for gay weddings.

In his speech to the Republican National Convention in 2016, fellow billionaire and entrepreneur Peter Thiel described this well when he said, "Of course, every American has a unique identity.... I am proud to be gay. I am proud to be a Republican. But most of all I am proud to be an American."[89] Exactly. What Trump is able to do to unite against the scourges of Western civilization is focus on those issues. Divisiveness can be sown only when the wounds have already been inflicted, a point that leftists refuse to acknowledge, even though that's really the only important thing we learned from the Russia debacle—that Russians were able to divide people with a couple grand's worth of Facebook ads. But people have to be wounded first by being told that supporting traditional marriage is hateful or that we cannot criticize sharia law or else we are homophobes, in order for divisiveness to develop. When Trump supports a political position, he finds a way to make it clear he is doing it out of joy, for love of country. Building the wall is not about keeping out legal immigrants who contribute to this country. It is about protecting Americans of all races, income levels, and backgrounds from the violence of some illegal immigrants and their coyotes and their drug trade. He wants to protect families from the despair of seeing their children murdered by illegal immigrants, like what happened to the Tibbetts and Steinle families. That is one reason he says "beautiful" so often; Trump's heart truly

[89] Will Drabold, "Read Peter Thiel's Speech at the Republican National Convention," *Time Magazine*, July 22, 2016, https://time.com/4417679/republican-convention-peter-thiel-transcript/.

breaks, I feel, when lives are prematurely ended by a preventable situation.

Churchill expressed similar sentiments in July 1940, as a German invasion loomed over Britain:

I stand at the head of a Government representing all parties in the State—all creeds, all classes, every recognizable section of opinion.… [T]here is one bond that unites us all and sustains us in the public regard…we are prepared to proceed to all extremities, to endure them, and to enforce them.… Thus only, in times like these, can nations preserve their freedom; and thus only can they uphold the cause entrusted to their care.… But all depends now upon the whole life-strength of the British race in every part of the world.… [L]et all strive without failing in faith or in duty; and the dark curse of Hitler will be lifted from our age.[90]

In other words, no matter someone's background, there is only one race that matters to Churchill, and that is the British race, made up of all people who live in Britain. Trump expressed similar sentiments in his July 4, 2019, speech called "Salute to America." You know it was a good speech because leftists hated it before it was given, then largely remained silent after he delivered it, proving them utterly and completely wrong.

In that speech, Trump eloquently says:

That same American spirit that emboldened our founders has kept us strong throughout our history. To this day, that spirit runs through the veins of every American patriot. It lives on in each and every one of you here today. It is the spirit of daring and defiance, excellence and adventure, courage

[90]   *Churchill: The Power of Words*, 261.

and confidence, loyalty and love that built this country into
the most exceptional nation in the history of the world, and
our nation is stronger today than it ever was before.... Two
hundred and fifty years ago, a volunteer army of farmers and
shopkeepers, blacksmiths, merchants, and militiamen risked
life and limb to secure American liberty and self-government.

This evening, we have witnessed the noble might of the
warriors who continue that legacy. They guard our birthright
with vigilance and fierce devotion to the flag and to our great
country.

Now we must go forward as a nation with that same unity
of purpose. As long as we stay true to our cause, as long as
we remember our great history, as long as we never ever stop
fighting for a better future, then there will be nothing that
America cannot do.[91]

Those words are the words of an American patriot, someone who loves his country and wants the best for his country.
He echoes the ebullience of George Washington, Ronald
Reagan, and countless other leaders who simply wanted the
best for their country, the same way parents want the best for
their children. In the same way, Churchill simply wanted the
best for his country of England, no matter what it took. It is with
ebullience that he took on the work of prime minister, so loving
his country that he returned to lead it after the British people
ungraciously refused to reelect him after he saved Europe and
Western civilization from near-certain ruin at the hands of fascism and communism. Likewise, Trump has saved Western

---

[91] Donald J. Trump, "Remarks by President Trump at a Salute to America,"
whitehouse.gov, July 5, 2019, https://www.whitehouse.gov/briefings-
statements/remarks-president-trump-salute-america/.

civilization from radical Islam, political correctness, a hatred of American values, and a hatred of America.

William Manchester echoes this point about Churchill's ebullience in *The Last Lion—Alone*. He writes:

> He had come to power because he had seen through Hitler from the very beginning—but not, ironically, because his inner light, the source of that insight, was understood by Englishmen. Churchill's star was invisible to the public and even to most of his peers. But a few saw it. One of them wrote afterward that although Winston knew the world was complex and in constant flux, to him "great things, races, and peoples, and morality were eternal."[92]

To put it another way, Winston understood the challenges facing the world, but he also knew that people are great and eternal, that they can face any foe presented to them. He had an ability to inspire people, even those who were not confident in themselves. Manchester continues:

> Churchill's mood seemed to confirm this. He possessed an inner radiance that year and felt it.... To him, Britain, "her message, and her glory, were very real.... He was instead the last of England's great Victorian statesmen, with views formed when the British lion's roar could silence the world; he was the champion of the Old Queen's realm and the defender and the protector of the values Englishmen of her reign had cherished, the principles they held inviolate, the vision which had illumined their world, which had steadied them in time of travail, and which he had embraced as a youth.

---

[92] *Last Lion—Alone*, 687.

Writing of his experience of being a prime minister, Churchill reflected on how he was joyful at the opportunity to seize the opportunity before him. He was ready to take on the challenges of being the leader of his country. He wrote, "Power, for the sake of lording it over fellow creatures, or adding to personal pomp, is rightly judged base. But power in a national crisis, when a man believes he knows what orders should be given is a blessing.... Ambition, not so much for vulgar ends, but for fame, glints in every mind.... An accepted leader has only to be sure of what it is best to do, or at least to have made up his mind about it."[93]

In other words, power can be tempting, but when power means the courage to act, and being trusted by the people to do so, it can be a great thing. Nevertheless, while Churchill remained joyful, he explained the double-edged sword that a leader always faces: "If he trips he must be sustained. If he makes mistakes they must be covered. If he sleeps he must not be wantonly disturbed. If he is no good he must be pole-axed."[94]

Trump faces a very similar dilemma every day. When he decides to bomb a place, you can be sure that within five minutes, the media will have a photo of a victim plastered on every station. But if he decides not to attack, or to halt an attack, the Max Boots of the world and the other neocons and war agitators will say that he is indecisive and cannot lead.

Clearly, Churchill and Trump are very similar in this way, as Trump is a tireless champion of American greatness and the will of the American people, with an ability to inspire the

---

[93] *Churchill: The Power of Words*, 241.
[94] *Churchill: The Power of Words*, 241.

downtrodden. Watch any Trump rally and you don't see your stereotypical country club Republicans in suits in the stands; you see average Americans of all backgrounds in the stands. You see people who love this country and are motivated by a desire to make America great again for all people. Signs like "Blacks for Trumps," "Vets for Trump," or "Women for Trump" are common sights at these rallies.

To emphasize how few people believed Trump would win (or wanted him to win), consider this: very few newspapers endorsed Trump for president, which is a badge of honor in that many in the media were very, very wrong about Trump.

In fact, the newspapers that endorsed him reflected the small-town support for him. The newspapers include the *Times-Gazette* (Hillsboro, Ohio; circulation of 4,300), the *Juneau Empire* (Juneau, Alaska; circulation of 7,500), and the *Waxahachie Daily Light* (Waxahachie, Texas; circulation of 3,191). But what did Trump care? He was speaking to the people and amassing free media coverage with every rally and tweet. Financial website TheStreet reported the amount of free media that Trump earned to be five billion dollars.[95]

Being the leader of the free world can be tough and demoralizing. Both Churchill and Trump had the weight of civilization on their shoulders, but they never once shrugged. Instead, like the great leaders they were, Churchill and Trump soldiered on with ebullience, projecting an optimism to the people they were

---

[95] Emily Stewart, "Donald Trump Rode $5 Billion in Free Media to the White House," TheStreet, November 20, 2016, https://www.thestreet.com/story/13896916/1/donald-trump-rode-5-billion-in-free-media-to-the-white-house.html.

leading as well as their enemies, who surely thought they would be demoralized.

For one final mention, these traits helped establish them as defenders of Western civilization.

CONCLUSION

In this book, I made two bold claims. One is that President Trump and Prime Minister Churchill have similar legacies, mainly how they saved Western civilization in their time. The second, bolder claim is that President Trump will be a greater defender of Western civilization than Churchill was. However, having reached the conclusion of this book, I feel confident in saying that I have defended my thesis. I have relied on contemporary and historical resources and analysis, and drawn on pages and pages of original source material. I have laid out factual arguments in a hopefully engaging and fun way. And although I used political language throughout this book and talked about "the left," I believe strongly that I have made my case. I'm sure the left-wingers in academia will be upset I didn't always use their high-minded Oxford language or didn't make my writing stuffy. But I wrote this book for everyone to be able to enjoy and appreciate the impact that Churchill and Trump had on our lives and on Western civilization.

The threats Churchill faced were Soviet aggression, communism, fascism, and a complacent Europe that dumbly let Germany become too aggressive and commit genocide, and then made a similar mistake in ignoring the threats posed by Stalin. If those threats hadn't been confronted, world history could have been permanently changed in a negative way forever, possibly leading to a world in which everyone had to live under the totalitarianism dictatorship of fascism or communism. Worse, racism would have thrived, and we would have returned to tribal warfare, as ethnic groups were split and pushed against one another.

Of fascism and Nazism, Churchill wrote these great lines and asked William Temple, the archbishop of Canterbury, to read them:

> *The systematic cruelties to which the Jewish people—men, women, and children—have been exposed under the Nazi regime are amongst the most terrible events of history, and place an indelible stain upon all who perpetrate and instigate them. Free men and women denounce these vile crimes, and when this world struggle ends with the enthronement of human rights, racial persecution will be ended.*[96]

It is clear optimism like this that is sorely needed in leaders of our day, and is often lacking in the weak and ineffectual leadership of people such as Angela Merkel and Barack Obama.

President Trump came into a country that was divided by heated racial rhetoric from President Obama, Black Lives Matter, and the fake news media. College campuses were being roiled by snowflakes and political correctness. Radical Islam was threatening safety and liberty in both the United States and overseas. A weak administration had allowed the Middle East to disintegrate and trust in the government to fall.

---

[96] *Churchill: The Power of Words*, 322.

But Donald Trump became president against all odds by employing a series of skills and characteristics. He connected to the average American through a shared patriotism and the ability to understand where they were coming from. He employed ebullience and intelligence to connect with normally divided groups, such as LGBT people and African Americans, by speaking to them about shared concerns. Furthermore, he is saving Western civilization by his prescience, forcing the fake news media and the Establishment to acknowledge issues like crime at the border, crime in the inner cities, and radical Islam. As I write this, he has somehow gotten Elijah Cummings, an African American representative from Baltimore, to go on the defensive over his record in his district and his failure on racial issues. When Trump tweets, people pay attention, and this is a skill Trump is using to save Western civilization.

This book has made many arguments in support of its thesis: that President Trump is the twenty-first-century defender of Western civilization in the same way that Prime Minister Churchill was the twentieth-century defender of Western civilization. I will repeat here what I have said many times throughout this book: President Donald Trump is going to be a greater defender of Western civilization than Prime Minister Winston Churchill was. I admire both men, I see both as serving an incredible role in saving Western civilization. In no way do I seek to diminish Churchill's accomplishments. In fact, without Churchill, Trump may not have been able to do what he did, as I've said previously. I believe that Churchill's leadership in fighting the Nazis and Soviet Union developed an important foreign policy handbook for dealing with threats to Western civilization, one that Trump has been able to replicate to defend

Western civilization from its own threats in the twenty-first century.

And as I have noted too, it's the reality of linear time that whoever comes after the other has the opportunity to be better than the person who came before; it's a fact of life and of time. Though Churchill did not directly teach Trump, of course, an analogy would be a professor who imparts all his wisdom to a student, and the student later goes on to advance that professor's research and make new discoveries. We should want better for the next generation, and Churchill, by fighting totalitarianism, apathy, a nation hungry for renewal, and weak leaders before him, gave Trump the playbook on how to do the same when he faced similar problems.

We know that Trump admires Churchill, but would Churchill have admired Trump? This is of course a bit of a dinner-party-game question, but I believe the answer is yes; Winston Churchill not only would have admired Trump but would have adored him. Churchill would have seen in Trump a strong desire to invest his personal life, which was already incredibly good when he was elected to be president, in saving America and encouraging the downtrodden men and women of America. These Americans had been demoralized by the feckless leadership of Barack Obama, the selling out of the American economy by the consultant class, and the destabilizing of American national security interests by the Council on Foreign Relations and the John Kerry/Hillary Clinton school of foreign policy.

He would have admired in President Trump his ability to set aside the personal attacks on him and the unending criticism and attacks claiming every ism and phobia known to man, in order to forge ahead with the plans he knows are right and true for restoring American greatness. He would have admired how President Trump is not afraid to name the enemies: radical Islam, racism, the deep state, the Establishment, and all others who profit from the destruction and misery of Americans. Churchill would have loved the way Trump handles the media and his political opponents, keeping them on their toes and making them reveal their true beliefs and hypocrisies. So yes, I do believe Churchill would have admired Trump.

I understand that not everyone reading this book will agree with all the assertions and arguments I make. But if you've gotten this far, you're at least open-minded and tolerant of arguments. I also understand that events can be difficult to judge in the moment. Nevertheless, I feel confident that if not now, in the future we will look back at what President Trump has accomplished and see him in the positive way we view Churchill regarding his role in saving Western civilization. Remember, Churchill, after saving his country from total ruin, and saving Europe, lost his reelection bid. Sometimes greatness and genius are not appreciated at the time.

Sometimes the traits we see in people that seem negative—brashness, boldness, a singular focus—are exactly what we need at the time. Sometimes we need a Samson, a David, a Churchill, a Trump to protect the great legacy of our people. It is with great honor that I hope I have encouraged a fresh look at the continuing legacy of both Prime Minister Churchill and President Trump, two great men who deserve a special place in history for defending the values of Western civilization. God bless this great country, and God bless Donald Trump.

APPENDIX A:
SPEECHES BY WINSTON CHURCHILL

"Disaster of the First Magnitude"
House of Commons, October 5, 1938
Addressing the Munich Agreement and British policy regarding Germany

I will begin by saying what everybody would like to ignore or forget but which must nevertheless be stated, namely, that we have sustained a total and unmitigated defeat, and that France has suffered even more than we have....

And I will say this, that I believe the Czechs, left to themselves and told they were going to get no help from the Western Powers, would have been able to make better terms than they have got—they could hardly have worse—after all this tremendous perturbation....

I have always held the view that the maintenance of peace depends upon the accumulation of deterrents against the aggressor, coupled with a sincere effort to redress grievances.... After [Hitler's] seizure of Austria in March...I ventured to appeal to the Government...to give a pledge that in conjunction with France and other Powers they would guarantee the security of

Czechoslovakia while the Sudeten-Deutsch question was being examined either by a League of Nations Commission or some other impartial body, and I still believe that if that course had been followed events would not have fallen into this disastrous state....

France and Great Britain together, especially if they had maintained a close contact with Russia, which certainly was not done, would have been able to influence many of the smaller States of Europe, and I believe they could have determined the attitude of Poland. Such a combination, prepared at a time when the German dictator was not deeply and irrevocably committed to his new adventure, would, I believe, have given strength to all those forces in Germany which resisted this departure, this new design.... Such action would have given strength to all that intense desire for peace, which the helpless German masses share with their British and French fellow men....

I do not think it is fair to charge those who wished to see this course followed, and followed consistently and resolutely, with having wished for an immediate war. Between submission and immediate war there was this third alternative, which gave a hope not only of peace but of justice. It is quite true that such a policy in order to succeed demanded that Britain should declare straight out and a long time beforehand that she would, with others, join to defend Czechoslovakia against an unprovoked aggression. His Majesty's Government refused to give that guarantee when it would have saved the situation....

All is over.... Czechoslovakia recedes into the darkness. She has suffered in every respect by her association with the Western democracies and with the League of Nations, of which she has always been an obedient servant. She has suffered in particular from her association with France, under whose guidance and policy she has been actuated for so long....

We in this country, as in other Liberal and democratic countries, have a perfect right to principle of self-determination, but it comes ill out of the mouths of those in totalitarian states who deny even the smallest element of toleration to every section and creed their bounds....

What is the remaining position of Czechoslovakia? Not only are they politically mutilated, but economically and financially, they complete confusion. Their banking, their railway arrangements, are severed and their industries are curtailed, and the movement of their population is most cruel.... It is a tragedy which has occurred....

I venture to think that in the future Czechoslovakian state cannot be maintained as an independent entity. You will find that in a period of time measured only by months, Czechoslovakia will be engulfed in the Nazi régime. Perhaps they may join it in despair or in revenge. At any rate, that story is over and told.... It is the most grievous consequence which we have yet experienced of what we have done and of what we have left undone in the last five years—five years of futile good intention, five years of eager search for the line of least resistance, five years of uninterrupted retreat of British power, five years neglect of our air defenses. We have been reduced from a position of security, of safety and power—power to do good, power to be generous to a beaten foe, power to make terms with Germany, power to give her proper redress for her grievances, power to stop her arming if we chose, power to take any step in strength or mercy or justice which we thought right—reduced in five years from a position safe and unchallenged to where we stand now.

When I think of the fair hopes of a long peace which still lay before Europe at the beginning of 1933 when Herr Hitler first obtained power, and of all the opportunities of arresting the growth of the Nazi power which have been thrown away, when I think of the immense combinations and resources which have been neglected or squandered, I cannot believe that a parallel exists in the whole course of history. So far as this country is concerned the responsibility must rest with those who have the undisputed control of our political affairs. They neither pre-vented Germany from rearming, nor did they rearm ourselves in time…. They neglected to make alliances and combinations which might have repaired previous errors, and thus they left us in the hour of trial without adequate national defense or effective international security….

We are in the presence of a disaster of the first magnitude…. Do not let us blind ourselves to that. It must now be accepted that all the countries of Central and Eastern Europe will make the best terms they can with the triumphant Nazi Power….

If the Nazi dictator should choose to look westward, as he may, bitterly will France and England regret the loss of that fine army of ancient Bohemia [Czechoslovakia] which was esti-mated last week to require not fewer than 30 German divisions for its destruction….

Many people, no doubt, honestly believe that they are only giving away the interests of Czechoslovakia, whereas I fear we shall find that we have deeply compromised, and perhaps fatally endangered, the safety and even the independence of Great Britain and France…. [T]here can never be friendship between the British democracy and the Nazi Power, that Power cannot ever be the trusted friend of the British democracy….

[O]ur loyal, brave people...should know the truth. They should know that there has been gross neglect and deficiency in our defenses; they should know that we have sustained a defeat without a war, the consequences of which will travel far with us along our road; they should know that we have passed an awful milestone in our history, when the whole equilibrium of Europe has been deranged, and that the terrible words have for the time being been pronounced against the Western democracies:

Thou art weighed in the balance and found wanting.

And do not suppose that this is the end. This is only the beginning of the reckoning.

Chancellor's Address
Bristol University, July 2, 1938

There are few words which are used more loosely than the word "Civilisation." What does it mean? It means a society based upon the opinion of civilians. It means that violence, the rule of warriors and despotic chiefs, the conditions of camps and warfare, of riot and tyranny, give place to parliaments where laws are made, and independent courts of justice in which over long periods those laws are maintained. That is Civilisation—and in its soil grow continually freedom, comfort, and culture. When Civilisation reigns in any country, a wider and less harassed life is afforded to the masses of the people. The traditions of the past are cherished, and the inheritance bequeathed to us by former wise or valiant men becomes a rich estate to be enjoyed and used by all.

The central principle of Civilisation is the subordination of the ruling authority to the settled customs of the people and to their will as expressed through the Constitution. In this Island we have today achieved in a high degree the blessings of Civilisation. There is freedom; there is law; there is love of country; there is a great measure of goodwill between classes; there is a widening prosperity. There are unmeasured opportunities of correcting abuses and making further progress.

In this very week we have seen a Prime Minister at the head of a large and loyal majority bow with good grace to the customs of Parliament, and we have heard Socialist Members speaking with pride of the precedents of the early seventeenth century, and the principles of the Petition of Right. In this respect for law and sense of continuity lies one of the glories of England. And more than that, there also lies in it an important part of her strength and safety. Such episodes are astonishing, but also educative, to countries where dictatorships prevail, and where no one dares to raise his hand against arbitrary power. They stir and cheer the minds of men in many lands.

We have, however, to face the problem of the turbulent, formidable world outside our shores. Why should not the same principles which have shaped the free, ordered, tolerant Civilisation of the British Isles and British Empire be found serviceable in the organisation of this anxious world? Why should not nations link themselves together in a larger system and establish a rule of law for the benefit of all? That surely is the supreme hope by which we should be inspired and the goal towards which we should march with resolute step.

But it is vain to imagine that the mere perception or declaration of right principles, whether in one country or for many countries, will be of any value unless they are supported by those qualities of civic virtue and manly courage—aye, and by those instruments and agencies of force and science which in the last resort must be the defence of right and reason.

Civilisation will not last, freedom will not survive, peace will not be kept, unless a very large majority of mankind unite together to defend them and show themselves possessed of a constabulary power before which barbaric and atavistic forces will stand in awe.

Here, then, we see the task which should command the exertions of the rising generation which fills this spacious hall, and which may bring to the life of Britain the surge of a new impulse towards the organization of world peace, and across the gulf of these eventful years prepare and bring nearer the Brotherhood of Man.

Liberty Day Meeting
Central Hall, Westminster, July 4, 1918

(Excerpted)

I move that the following resolution be cabled from the meeting as a greeting to the President and people of the United States of America: This meeting of the Anglo-Saxon Fellowship assembled in London on the 4th of July, 1918, send to the President and people of the United States their heartfelt greetings on the 142nd anniversary of the Declaration of American Independence. They rejoice that the love of liberty and justice on which the American nation was founded should in the present time of trial have united the whole English-speaking family in a brotherhood of arms.

We are met here today at Westminster to celebrate the national festival of the American people and the 142nd anniversary of the Declaration of Independence. We are met here also as brothers-in-arms facing for a righteous cause grave injuries and perils and passing through times of exceptional anxiety and suffering. We therefore seek to draw from the past history of our race inspiration and comfort to cheer our hearts and fortify and purify our resolution and our comradeship.

A great harmony exists between the spirit and language of the Declaration of Independence and all we are fighting for now. A similar harmony exists between the principles of that Declaration and all that the British people have wished to stand for, and have in fact achieved at last both here at home and in the self-governing Dominions of the Crown.

The Declaration of Independence is not only an American document. It follows on Magna Carta and the Bill of Rights as the third great title-deed on which the liberties of the English-speaking people are founded. By it we lost an Empire, but by it we also preserved an Empire. By applying its principles and learning its lesson we have maintained our communion with the powerful Commonwealths our children have established beyond the seas.

Wherever men seek to frame politics or constitutions which safeguard the citizen, be he rich or poor, on the one hand from the shame of despotism, on the other from the miseries of anarchy, which combine personal freedom with respect for law and love of country, it is to the inspiration which originally sprang from the English soil and from the Anglo-Saxon mind that they will inevitably recur. We therefore join in perfect sincerity and simplicity with our American kith and kin in celebrating the auspicious and glorious anniversary of their nationhood.

APPENDIX B:
SPEECHES BY DONALD TRUMP

Presidential Inauguration
January 20, 2017

(As prepared for delivery)

Chief Justice Roberts, President Carter, President Clinton, President Bush, President Obama, fellow Americans, and people of the world: thank you.

We, the citizens of America, are now joined in a great national effort to rebuild our country and to restore its promise for all of our people.

Together, we will determine the course of America and the world for years to come.

We will face challenges. We will confront hardships. But we will get the job done.

Every four years, we gather on these steps to carry out the orderly and peaceful transfer of power, and we are grateful to President Obama and First Lady Michelle Obama for their gracious aid throughout this transition. They have been magnificent.

Today's ceremony, however, has very special meaning. Because today we are not merely transferring power from one

Administration to another, or from one party to another—but we are transferring power from Washington, D.C. and giving it back to you, the American People.

For too long, a small group in our nation's Capital has reaped the rewards of government while the people have borne the cost.

Washington flourished—but the people did not share in its wealth.

Politicians prospered—but the jobs left, and the factories closed.

The establishment protected itself, but not the citizens of our country.

Their victories have not been your victories; their triumphs have not been your triumphs; and while they celebrated in our nation's Capital, there was little to celebrate for struggling families all across our land.

That all changes—starting right here, and right now, because this moment is your moment: it belongs to you.

It belongs to everyone gathered here today and everyone watching all across America.

This is your day. This is your celebration.

And this, the United States of America, is your country.

What truly matters is not which party controls our government, but whether our government is controlled by the people.

January 20th 2017, will be remembered as the day the people became the rulers of this nation again.

The forgotten men and women of our country will be forgotten no longer.

Everyone is listening to you now.

You came by the tens of millions to become part of a historic movement the likes of which the world has never seen before.

At the center of this movement is a crucial conviction: that a nation exists to serve its citizens.

Americans want great schools for their children, safe neighborhoods for their families, and good jobs for themselves.

These are the just and reasonable demands of a righteous public.

But for too many of our citizens, a different reality exists: Mothers and children trapped in poverty in our inner cities; rusted-out factories scattered like tombstones across the landscape of our nation; an education system, flush with cash, but which leaves our young and beautiful students deprived of knowledge; and the crime and gangs and drugs that have stolen too many lives and robbed our country of so much unrealized potential.

This American carnage stops right here and stops right now.

We are one nation—and their pain is our pain. Their dreams are our dreams; and their success will be our success. We share one heart, one home, and one glorious destiny.

The oath of office I take today is an oath of allegiance to all Americans.

For many decades, we've enriched foreign industry at the expense of American industry;

Subsidized the armies of other countries while allowing for the very sad depletion of our military;

We've defended other nation's borders while refusing to defend our own;

And spent trillions of dollars overseas while America's infrastructure has fallen into disrepair and decay.

We've made other countries rich while the wealth, strength, and confidence of our country has disappeared over the horizon.

One by one, the factories shuttered and left our shores, with not even a thought about the millions upon millions of American workers left behind.

The wealth of our middle class has been ripped from their homes and then redistributed across the entire world.

But that is the past. And now we are looking only to the future.

We assembled here today are issuing a new decree to be heard in every city, in every foreign capital, and in every hall of power.

From this day forward, a new vision will govern our land.

From this moment on, it's going to be America First.

Every decision on trade, on taxes, on immigration, on foreign affairs, will be made to benefit American workers and American families.

We must protect our borders from the ravages of other countries making our products, stealing our companies, and destroying our jobs. Protection will lead to great prosperity and strength.

I will fight for you with every breath in my body—and I will never, ever let you down.

America will start winning again, winning like never before.

We will bring back our jobs. We will bring back our borders. We will bring back our wealth. And we will bring back our dreams.

We will build new roads, and highways, and bridges, and airports, and tunnels, and railways all across our wonderful nation.

We will get our people off of welfare and back to work—rebuilding our country with American hands and American labor.

We will follow two simple rules: Buy American and Hire American.

We will seek friendship and goodwill with the nations of the world—but we do so with the understanding that it is the right of all nations to put their own interests first.

We do not seek to impose our way of life on anyone, but rather to let it shine as an example for everyone to follow.

We will reinforce old alliances and form new ones—and unite the civilized world against Radical Islamic Terrorism, which we will eradicate completely from the face of the Earth.

At the bedrock of our politics will be a total allegiance to the United States of America, and through our loyalty to our country, we will rediscover our loyalty to each other.

When you open your heart to patriotism, there is no room for prejudice.

The Bible tells us, "how good and pleasant it is when God's people live together in unity."

We must speak our minds openly, debate our disagreements honestly, but always pursue solidarity.

When America is united, America is totally unstoppable.

There should be no fear—we are protected, and we will always be protected.

We will be protected by the great men and women of our military and law enforcement and, most importantly, we are protected by God.

Finally, we must think big and dream even bigger.

In America, we understand that a nation is only living as long as it is striving.

We will no longer accept politicians who are all talk and no action—constantly complaining but never doing anything about it.

The time for empty talk is over.

Now arrives the hour of action.

Do not let anyone tell you it cannot be done. No challenge can match the heart and fight and spirit of America.

We will not fail. Our country will thrive and prosper again.

We stand at the birth of a new millennium, ready to unlock the mysteries of space, to free the Earth from the miseries of disease, and to harness the energies, industries and technologies of tomorrow.

A new national pride will stir our souls, lift our sights, and heal our divisions.

It is time to remember that old wisdom our soldiers will never forget: that whether we are black or brown or white, we all bleed the same red blood of patriots, we all enjoy the same glorious freedoms, and we all salute the same great American Flag.

And whether a child is born in the urban sprawl of Detroit or the windswept plains of Nebraska, they look up at the same night sky, they fill their heart with the same dreams, and they are infused with the breath of life by the same almighty Creator.

So to all Americans, in every city near and far, small and large, from mountain to mountain, and from ocean to ocean, hear these words:

You will never be ignored again.

Your voice, your hopes, and your dreams, will define our American destiny. And your courage and goodness and love will forever guide us along the way.

Together, We Will Make America Strong Again.

We Will Make America Wealthy Again.

We Will Make America Proud Again.

We Will Make America Safe Again.

And, Yes, Together, We Will Make America Great Again. Thank you, God Bless You, And God Bless America.

On Western Civilization
Krasiński Square, Warsaw, Poland, July 6, 2017

Mrs. Trump: Hello, Poland! Thank you very much. My husband and I have enjoyed visiting your beautiful country. I want to thank President and Mrs. Duda for the warm welcome and their generous hospitality. I had the opportunity to visit the Copernicus Science Centre today, and found it not only informative but thoughtful, its mission, which is to inspire people to observe, experiment, ask questions, and seek answers.

I can think of no better purpose for such a wonderful science center. Thank you to all who were involved in giving us the tour, especially the children who made it such a wonderful experience.

As many of you know, a main focus of my husband's presidency is safety and security of the American people. I think all of us can agree people should be able to live their lives without fear, no matter what country they live in. That is my wish for all of us around the world. (Applause.)

Thank you again for this wonderful welcome to your very special country. Your kindness and gracious hospitality will not be forgotten. (Applause.)

And now it is my honor to introduce to you my husband, the President of the United States, Donald J. Trump. (Applause.)

President Trump: Thank you very much. That's so nice. The United States has many great diplomats, but there is truly no better ambassador for our country than our beautiful First Lady, Melania. Thank you, Melania. That was very nice. (Applause.)

We've come to your nation to deliver a very important message: America loves Poland, and America loves the Polish people. (Applause.) Thank you.

The Poles have not only greatly enriched this region, but Polish-Americans have also greatly enriched the United States, and I was truly proud to have their support in the 2016 election. (Applause.)

It is a profound honor to stand in this city, by this monument to the Warsaw Uprising, and to address the Polish nation that so many generations have dreamed of: a Poland that is safe, strong, and free. (Applause.)

President Duda and your wonderful First Lady, Agata, have welcomed us with the tremendous warmth and kindness for which Poland is known around the world. Thank you. (Applause.) My sincere—and I mean sincerely thank both of them. And to Prime Minister Syzdlo, a very special thanks also. (Applause.)

We are also pleased that former President Lech Walesa, so famous for leading the Solidarity Movement, has joined us today, also. (Applause.) Thank you. Thank you. Thank you.

On behalf of all Americans, let me also thank the entire Polish people for the generosity you have shown in welcoming our soldiers to your country. These soldiers are not only brave defenders of freedom, but also symbols of America's commitment to your security and your place in a strong and democratic Europe.

We are proudly joined on stage by American, Polish, British, and Romanian soldiers. Thank you. (Applause.) Thank you. Great job.

President Duda and I have just come from an incredibly successful meeting with the leaders participating in the Three Seas Initiative. To the citizens of this great region, America is eager to expand our partnership with you. We welcome stronger ties of trade and commerce as you grow your economies. And we are committed to securing your access to alternate sources of energy, so Poland and its neighbors are never again held hostage to a single supplier of energy. (Applause.)

Mr. President, I congratulate you, along with the President of Croatia, on your leadership of this historic Three Seas Initiative. Thank you. (Applause.)

This is my first visit to Central Europe as President, and I am thrilled that it could be right here at this magnificent, beautiful piece of land. It is beautiful. (Applause.) Poland is the geographic heart of Europe, but more importantly, in the Polish people, we see the soul of Europe. Your nation is great because your spirit is great and your spirit is strong. (Applause.)

For two centuries, Poland suffered constant and brutal attacks. But while Poland could be invaded and occupied, and its borders even erased from the map, it could never be erased from history or from your hearts. In those dark days, you have lost your land but you never lost your pride. (Applause.)

So it is with true admiration that I can say today, that from the farms and villages of your countryside to the cathedrals and squares of your great cities, Poland lives, Poland prospers, and Poland prevails. (Applause.)

Despite every effort to transform you, oppress you, or destroy you, you endured and overcame. You are the proud nation of Copernicus—think of that—(applause)—Chopin, Saint John Paul II. Poland is a land of great heroes. (Applause.) And you are a people who know the true value of what you defend.

The triumph of the Polish spirit over centuries of hardship gives us all hope for a future in which good conquers evil, and peace achieves victory over war.

For Americans, Poland has been a symbol of hope since the beginning of our nation. Polish heroes and American patriots fought side by side in our War of Independence and in many wars that followed. Our soldiers still serve together today in Afghanistan and Iraq, combatting the enemies of all civilization.

For America's part, we have never given up on freedom and independence as the right and destiny of the Polish people, and we never, ever will. (Applause.)

Our two countries share a special bond forged by unique histories and national characters. It's a fellowship that exists only among people who have fought and bled and died for freedom. (Applause.)

The signs of this friendship stand in our nation's capital. Just steps from the White House, we've raised statues of men with names like Pułaski and Kościuszko. (Applause.) The same is true in Warsaw, where street signs carry the name of George Washington, and a monument stands to one of the world's greatest heroes, Ronald Reagan. (Applause.)

And so I am here today not just to visit an old ally, but to hold it up as an example for others who seek freedom and who wish to summon the courage and the will to defend our civilization. (Applause.) The story of Poland is the story of a people who have never lost hope, who have never been broken, and who have never, ever forgotten who they are. (Applause)

Audience: Donald Trump! Donald Trump! Donald Trump!

President Trump: Thank you. Thank you so much. Thank you. Thank you so much. Such a great honor. This is a nation more than one thousand years old. Your borders were erased for more than a century and only restored just one century ago.

In 1920, in the Miracle of Vistula, Poland stopped the Soviet army bent on European conquest. (Applause.) Then, 19 years later in 1939, you were invaded yet again, this time by Nazi Germany from the west and the Soviet Union from the east. That's trouble. That's tough.

Under a double occupation the Polish people endured evils beyond description: the Katyn forest massacre, the occupations, the Holocaust, the Warsaw Ghetto and the Warsaw Ghetto Uprising, the destruction of this beautiful capital city, and the deaths of nearly one in five Polish people. A vibrant Jewish population—the largest in Europe—was reduced to almost nothing after the Nazis systematically murdered millions of Poland's Jewish citizens, along with countless others, during that brutal occupation.

In the summer of 1944, the Nazi and Soviet armies were preparing for a terrible and bloody battle right here in Warsaw. Amid that hell on earth, the citizens of Poland rose up to defend their homeland. I am deeply honored to be joined on stage today by veterans and heroes of the Warsaw Uprising. (Applause.)

Audience: (Chanting.)

President Trump: What great spirit. We salute your noble sacrifice and we pledge to always remember your fight for Poland and for freedom. Thank you. Thank you. (Applause.)

This monument reminds us that more than 150,000 Poles died during that desperate struggle to overthrow oppression.

From the other side of the river, the Soviet armed forces stopped and waited. They watched as the Nazis ruthlessly destroyed the city, viciously murdering men, women, and children. They tried to destroy this nation forever by shattering its will to survive.

But there is a courage and a strength deep in the Polish character that no one could destroy. The Polish martyr, Bishop Michael Kozal, said it well: "More horrifying than a defeat of arms is a collapse of the human spirit."

Through four decades of communist rule, Poland and the other captive nations of Europe endured a brutal campaign to demolish freedom, your faith, your laws, your history, your identity—indeed the very essence of your culture and your humanity. Yet, through it all, you never lost that spirit. (Applause.) Your oppressors tried to break you, but Poland could not be broken. (Applause.)

And when the day came on June 2nd, 1979, and one million Poles gathered around Victory Square for their very first mass with their Polish Pope, that day, every communist in Warsaw must have known that their oppressive system would soon come crashing down. (Applause.) They must have known it at the exact moment during Pope John Paul II's sermon when a million Polish men, women, and children suddenly raised their voices in a single prayer. A million Polish people did not ask for wealth. They did not ask for privilege. Instead, one million Poles sang three simple words: "We want God." (Applause.)

In those words, the Polish people recalled the promise of a better future. They found new courage to face down their oppressors, and they found the words to declare that Poland would be Poland once again.

As I stand here today before this incredible crowd, this faithful nation, we can still hear those voices that echo through history. Their message is as true today as ever. The people of Poland, the people of America, and the people of Europe still cry out "We want God." (Applause.)

Together, with Pope John Paul II, the Poles reasserted their identity as a nation devoted to God. And with that powerful declaration of who you are, you came to understand what to do and how to live. You stood in solidarity against oppression, against a lawless secret police, against a cruel and wicked system that impoverished your cities and your souls. And you won. Poland prevailed. Poland will always prevail. (Applause.)

Audience: Donald Trump! Donald Trump! Donald Trump!

President Trump: Thank you. You were supported in that victory over communism by a strong alliance of free nations in the West that defied tyranny. Now, among the most committed members of the NATO Alliance, Poland has resumed its place as a leading nation of a Europe that is strong, whole, and free.

A strong Poland is a blessing to the nations of Europe, and they know that. A strong Europe is a blessing to the West and to the world. (Applause.) One hundred years after the entry of American forces into World War I, the transatlantic bond between the United States and Europe is as strong as ever and maybe, in many ways, even stronger.

This continent no longer confronts the specter of communism. But today we're in the West, and we have to say there are dire threats to our security and to our way of life. You see what's happening out there. They are threats. We will confront them. We will win. But they are threats. (Applause.)

Audience: Donald Trump! Donald Trump! Donald Trump!

President Trump: We are confronted by another oppressive ideology—one that seeks to export terrorism and extremism all around the globe. America and Europe have suffered one terror attack after another. We're going to get it to stop. (Applause.)

During a historic gathering in Saudi Arabia, I called on the leaders of more than 50 Muslim nations to join together to drive out this menace which threatens all of humanity. We must stand united against these shared enemies to strip them of their territory and their funding, and their networks, and any form of ideological support that they may have. While we will always welcome new citizens who share our values and love our people, our borders will always be closed to terrorism and extremism of any kind. (Applause.)

Audience: Donald Trump! Donald Trump! Donald Trump!

President Trump: We are fighting hard against radical Islamic terrorism, and we will prevail. We cannot accept those who reject our values and who use hatred to justify violence against the innocent.

Today, the West is also confronted by the powers that seek to test our will, undermine our confidence, and challenge our interests. To meet new forms of aggression, including propaganda, financial crimes, and cyberwarfare, we must adapt our alliance to compete effectively in new ways and on all new battlefields.

We urge Russia to cease its destabilizing activities in Ukraine and elsewhere, and its support for hostile regimes—including Syria and Iran—and to instead join the community of responsible nations in our fight against common enemies and in defense of civilization itself. (Applause.)

Finally, on both sides of the Atlantic, our citizens are confronted by yet another danger—one firmly within our control. This danger is invisible to some but familiar to the Poles: the steady creep of government bureaucracy that drains the vitality and wealth of the people. The West became great not because of paperwork and regulations but because people were allowed to chase their dreams and pursue their destinies.

Americans, Poles, and the nations of Europe value individual freedom and sovereignty. We must work together to confront forces, whether they come from inside or out, from the South or the East, that threaten over time to undermine these values and to erase the bonds of culture, faith and tradition that make us who we are. (Applause.) If left unchecked, these forces will undermine our courage, sap our spirit, and weaken our will to defend ourselves and our societies.

But just as our adversaries and enemies of the past learned here in Poland, we know that these forces, too, are doomed to fail if we want them to fail. And we do, indeed, want them to fail. (Applause.) They are doomed not only because our alliance is strong, our countries are resilient, and our power is unmatched. Through all of that, you have to say everything is true. Our adversaries, however, are doomed because we will never forget who we are. And if we don't forget who are, we just can't be beaten. Americans will never forget. The nations of Europe will never forget. We are the fastest and the greatest community. There is nothing like our community of nations. The world has never known anything like our community of nations.

We write symphonies. We pursue innovation. We celebrate our ancient heroes, embrace our timeless traditions and customs, and always seek to explore and discover brand-new frontiers.

We reward brilliance. We strive for excellence, and cherish inspiring works of art that honor God. We treasure the rule of law and protect the right to free speech and free expression. (Applause.)

We empower women as pillars of our society and of our success. We put faith and family, not government and bureaucracy, at the center of our lives. And we debate everything. We challenge everything. We seek to know everything so that we can better know ourselves. (Applause.)

And above all, we value the dignity of every human life, protect the rights of every person, and share the hope of every soul to live in freedom. That is who we are. Those are the priceless ties that bind us together as nations, as allies, and as a civilization.

What we have, what we inherited from our—and you know this better than anybody, and you see it today with this incredible group of people—what we've inherited from our ancestors has never existed to this extent before. And if we fail to preserve it, it will never, ever exist again. So we cannot fail.

This great community of nations has something else in common: In every one of them, it is the people, not the powerful, who have always formed the foundation of freedom and the cornerstone of our defense. The people have been that foundation here in Poland—as they were right here in Warsaw—and they were the foundation from the very, very beginning in America.

Our citizens did not win freedom together, did not survive horrors together, did not face down evil together, only to lose our freedom to a lack of pride and confidence in our values. We did not and we will not. We will never back down. (Applause.)

Audience: Donald Trump! Donald Trump! Donald Trump!

President Trump: As long as we know our history, we will know how to build our future. Americans know that a strong alliance of free, sovereign and independent nations is the best defense for our freedoms and for our interests. That is why my administration has demanded that all members of NATO finally meet their full and fair financial obligation.

As a result of this insistence, billions of dollars more have begun to pour into NATO. In fact, people are shocked. But billions and billions of dollars more are coming in from countries that, in my opinion, would not have been paying so quickly.

To those who would criticize our tough stance, I would point out that the United States has demonstrated not merely with words but with its actions that we stand firmly behind Article 5, the mutual defense commitment. (Applause.)

Words are easy, but actions are what matters. And for its own protection—and you know this, everybody knows this, everybody has to know this—Europe must do more. Europe must demonstrate that it believes in its future by investing its money to secure that future.

That is why we applaud Poland for its decision to move forward this week on acquiring from the United States the battle-tested Patriot air and missile defense system—the best anywhere in the world. (Applause.) That is also why we salute the Polish people for being one of the NATO countries that has actually achieved the benchmark for investment in our common defense. Thank you. Thank you, Poland. I must tell you, the example you set is truly magnificent, and we applaud Poland. Thank you. (Applause.)

We have to remember that our defense is not just a commitment of money, it is a commitment of will. Because as the Polish experience reminds us, the defense of the West ultimately rests not only on means but also on the will of its people to prevail and be successful and get what you have to have. The fundamental question of our time is whether the West has the will to survive. Do we have the confidence in our values to defend them at any cost? Do we have enough respect for our citizens to protect our borders? Do we have the desire and the courage to preserve our civilization in the face of those who would subvert and destroy it? (Applause.)

We can have the largest economies and the most lethal weapons anywhere on Earth, but if we do not have strong families and strong values, then we will be weak and we will not survive. (Applause.) If anyone forgets the critical importance of these things, let them come to one country that never has. Let them come to Poland. (Applause.) And let them come here, to Warsaw, and learn the story of the Warsaw Uprising.

When they do, they should learn about Jerusalem Avenue. In August of 1944, Jerusalem Avenue was one of the main roads running east and west through this city, just as it is today.

Control of that road was crucially important to both sides in the battle for Warsaw. The German military wanted it as their most direct route to move troops and to form a very strong front. And for the Polish Home Army, the ability to pass north and south across that street was critical to keep the center of the city, and the Uprising itself, from being split apart and destroyed.

Every night, the Poles put up sandbags amid machine gun fire—and it was horrendous fire—to protect a narrow passage across Jerusalem Avenue. Every day, the enemy forces knocked them down again and again and again. Then the Poles dug a trench. Finally, they built a barricade. And the brave Polish fighters began to flow across Jerusalem Avenue. That narrow passageway, just a few feet wide, was the fragile link that kept the Uprising alive.

Between its walls, a constant stream of citizens and freedom fighters made their perilous, just perilous, sprints. They ran across that street, they ran through that street, they ran under that street—all to defend this city. "The far side was several yards away," recalled one young Polish woman named Greta. That mortality and that life was so important to her. In fact, she said, "The mortally dangerous sector of the street was soaked in the blood. It was the blood of messengers, liaison girls, and couriers."

Nazi snipers shot at anybody who crossed. Anybody who crossed, they were being shot at. Their soldiers burned every building on the street, and they used the Poles as human shields for their tanks in their effort to capture Jerusalem Avenue. The enemy never ceased its relentless assault on that small outpost of civilization. And the Poles never ceased its defense.

The Jerusalem Avenue passage required constant protection, repair, and reinforcement, but the will of its defenders did not waver, even in the face of death. And to the last days of the Uprising, the fragile crossing never, ever failed. It was never, ever forgotten. It was kept open by the Polish people.

The memories of those who perished in the Warsaw Uprising cry out across the decades, and few are clearer than the memories of those who died to build and defend the Jerusalem Avenue crossing. Those heroes remind us that the West was saved with the blood of patriots; that each generation must rise up and play their part in its defense—(applause)—and that every foot of ground, and every last inch of civilization, is worth defending with your life.

Our own fight for the West does not begin on the battlefield—it begins with our minds, our wills, and our souls. Today, the ties that unite our civilization are no less vital, and demand no less defense, than that bare shred of land on which the hope of Poland once totally rested. Our freedom, our civilization, and our survival depend on these bonds of history, culture, and memory.

And today as ever, Poland is in our heart, and its people are in that fight. (Applause.) Just as Poland could not be broken, I declare today for the world to hear that the West will never, ever be broken. Our values will prevail. Our people will thrive. And our civilization will triumph. (Applause.)

Audience: Donald Trump! Donald Trump! Donald Trump!

President Trump: Thank you. So, together, let us all fight like the Poles—for family, for freedom, for country, and for God.

Thank you. God Bless You. God bless the Polish people. God bless our allies. And God bless the United States of America.

Thank you. God bless you. Thank you very much. (Applause.)

State of the Union
U.S. Congress, February 5, 2019

President Trump: Madam Speaker, Mr. Vice President, Members of Congress, the First Lady of the United States—(applause)—and my fellow Americans:

We meet tonight at a moment of unlimited potential. As we begin a new Congress, I stand here ready to work with you to achieve historic breakthroughs for all Americans.

Millions of our fellow citizens are watching us now, gathered in this great chamber, hoping that we will govern not as two parties but as one nation. (Applause.)

The agenda I will lay out this evening is not a Republican agenda or a Democrat agenda. It's the agenda of the American people.

Many of us have campaigned on the same core promises: to defend American jobs and demand fair trade for American workers; to rebuild and revitalize our nation's infrastructure; to reduce the price of healthcare and prescription drugs; to create an immigration system that is safe, lawful, modern, and secure; and to pursue a foreign policy that puts America's interests first.

There is a new opportunity in American politics, if only we have the courage, together, to seize it. (Applause.) Victory is not winning for our party. Victory is winning for our country. (Applause.)

This year, America will recognize two important anniversaries that show us the majesty of America's mission and the power of American pride.

In June, we mark 75 years since the start of what General Dwight D. Eisenhower called the "Great Crusade"—the Allied liberation of Europe in World War II. (Applause.) On D-Day, June 6th, 1944, 15,000 young American men jumped from the sky, and 60,000 more stormed in from the sea, to save our civilization from tyranny. Here with us tonight are three of those incredible heroes: Private First Class Joseph Reilly, Staff Sergeant Irving Locker, and Sergeant Herman Zeitchik. (Applause.) Please. Gentlemen, we salute you.

In 2019, we also celebrate 50 years since brave young pilots flew a quarter of a million miles through space to plant the American flag on the face of the moon. Half a century later, we are joined by one of the Apollo 11 astronauts who planted that flag: Buzz Aldrin. (Applause.) Thank you, Buzz. This year, American astronauts will go back to space on American rockets. (Applause.)

In the 20th century, America saved freedom, transformed science, redefined the middle class, and, when you get down to it, there's nothing anywhere in the world that can compete with America. (Applause.) Now we must step boldly and bravely into the next chapter of this great American adventure, and we must create a new standard of living for the 21st century. An amazing quality of life for all of our citizens is within reach.

We can make our communities safer, our families stronger, our culture richer, our faith deeper, and our middle class bigger and more prosperous than ever before. (Applause.)

But we must reject the politics of revenge, resistance, and retribution, and embrace the boundless potential of cooperation, compromise, and the common good. (Applause.)

Together, we can break decades of political stalemate. We can bridge old divisions, heal old wounds, build new coalitions, forge new solutions, and unlock the extraordinary promise of America's future. The decision is ours to make.

We must choose between greatness or gridlock, results or resistance, vision or vengeance, incredible progress or pointless destruction.

Tonight, I ask you to choose greatness. (Applause.)

Over the last two years, my administration has moved with urgency and historic speed to confront problems neglected by leaders of both parties over many decades.

In just over two years since the election, we have launched an unprecedented economic boom—a boom that has rarely been seen before. There's been nothing like it. We have created 5.3 million new jobs and, importantly, added 600,000 new manufacturing jobs—something which almost everyone said was impossible to do. But the fact is, we are just getting started. (Applause.)

Wages are rising at the fastest pace in decades and growing for blue-collar workers, who I promised to fight for. They're growing faster than anyone else thought possible. Nearly 5 million Americans have been lifted off food stamps. (Applause.)

The U.S. economy is growing almost twice as fast today as when I took office. And we are considered, far and away, the hottest economy anywhere in the world. Not even close. (Applause.)

Unemployment has reached the lowest rate in over half a century. (Applause.) African American, Hispanic American, and Asian American unemployment have all reached their lowest levels ever recorded. (Applause.) Unemployment for Americans with disabilities has also reached an all-time low. (Applause.) More people are working now than at any time in the history of our country—157 million people at work. (Applause.)

We passed a massive tax cut for working families and doubled the child tax credit. (Applause.)

We virtually ended the estate tax—or death tax, as it is often called—on small businesses for ranchers and also for family farms. (Applause.)

We eliminated the very unpopular Obamacare individual mandate penalty. (Applause.) And to give critically ill patients access to lifesaving cures, we passed, very importantly, Right to Try. (Applause.)

My administration has cut more regulations in a short period of time than any other administration during its entire tenure. (Applause.) Companies are coming back to our country in large numbers thanks to our historic reductions in taxes and regulations. (Applause.)

And we have unleashed a revolution in American energy. The United States is now the number-one producer of oil and natural gas anywhere in the world. (Applause.) And now, for the first time in 65 years, we are a net exporter of energy. (Applause.)

After 24 months of rapid progress, our economy is the envy of the world, our military is the most powerful on Earth, by far, and America—(applause)—America is again winning each and every day. (Applause.)

Members of Congress: The state of our union is strong. (Applause.)

Audience: USA! USA! USA!

President Trump: That sounds so good. (Laughter.)

Our country is vibrant and our economy is thriving like never before.

On Friday, it was announced that we added another 304,000 jobs last month alone—almost double the number expected. (Applause.) An economic miracle is taking place in the United States, and the only thing that can stop it are foolish wars, politics, or ridiculous partisan investigations. (Applause.)

If there is going to be peace and legislation, there cannot be war and investigation. It just doesn't work that way.

We must be united at home to defeat our adversaries abroad. This new era of cooperation can start with finally confirming the more than 300 highly qualified nominees who are still stuck in the Senate. In some cases, years and years waiting. Not right. (Applause.) The Senate has failed to act on these nominations, which is unfair to the nominees and very unfair to our country.

Now is the time for bipartisan action. Believe it or not, we have already proven that that's possible.

In the last Congress, both parties came together to pass unprecedented legislation to confront the opioid crisis, a sweeping new farm bill, historic VA reforms. And after four decades of rejection, we passed VA Accountability so that we can finally terminate those who mistreat our wonderful veterans. (Applause.)

And just weeks ago, both parties united for groundbreaking criminal justice reform. They said it couldn't be done. (Applause.)

Last year, I heard, through friends, the story of Alice Johnson. I was deeply moved. In 1997, Alice was sentenced to life in prison as a first-time non-violent drug offender. Over the next 22 years, she became a prison minister, inspiring others to choose a better path. She had a big impact on that prison population, and far beyond.

Alice's story underscores the disparities and unfairness that can exist in criminal sentencing, and the need to remedy this total injustice. She served almost that 22 years and had expected to be in prison for the remainder of her life.

In June, I commuted Alice's sentence. When I saw Alice's beautiful family greet her at the prison gates, hugging and kissing and crying and laughing, I knew I did something right. Alice is with us tonight, and she is a terrific woman. Terrific. Alice, please. (Applause.)

Alice, thank you for reminding us that we always have the power to shape our own destiny. Thank you very much, Alice. Thank you very much. (Applause.)

Inspired by stories like Alice's, my administration worked closely with members of both parties to sign the FIRST STEP Act into law. Big deal. (Applause.) It's a big deal.

This legislation reformed sentencing laws that have wrongly and disproportionately harmed the African American community. The FIRST STEP Act gives non-violent offenders the chance to reenter society as productive, law-abiding citizens. Now states across the country are following our lead. America is a nation that believes in redemption.

We are also joined tonight by Matthew Charles from Tennessee. In 1996, at the age of 30, Matthew was sentenced to 35 years for selling drugs and related offenses. Over the next two decades, he completed more than 30 Bible studies, became a law clerk, and mentored many of his fellow inmates.

Now, Matthew is the very first person to be released from prison under the FIRST STEP Act. (Applause.) Matthew, please. Thank you, Matthew. Welcome home. (Applause.)

Now, Republicans and Democrats must join forces again to confront an urgent national crisis. Congress has 10 days left to pass a bill that will fund our government, protect our homeland, and secure our very dangerous southern border.

Now is the time for Congress to show the world that America is committed to ending illegal immigration and putting the ruthless coyotes, cartels, drug dealers, and human traffickers out of business. (Applause.)

As we speak, large, organized caravans are on the march to the United States. We have just heard that Mexican cities, in order to remove the illegal immigrants from their communities, are getting trucks and buses to bring them up to our country in areas where there is little border protection. I have ordered another 3,750 troops to our southern border to prepare for this tremendous onslaught.

This is a moral issue. The lawless state of our southern border is a threat to the safety, security, and financial wellbeing of all America. We have a moral duty to create an immigration system that protects the lives and jobs of our citizens. This includes our obligation to the millions of immigrants living here today who followed the rules and respected our laws. Legal immigrants enrich our nation and strengthen our society in countless ways. (Applause.)

I want people to come into our country in the largest numbers ever, but they have to come in legally. (Applause.)

Tonight, I am asking you to defend our very dangerous southern border out of love and devotion to our fellow citizens and to our country.

No issue better illustrates the divide between America's working class and America's political class than illegal immigration. Wealthy politicians and donors push for open borders while living their lives behind walls, and gates, and guards. (Applause.)

Meanwhile, working-class Americans are left to pay the price for mass illegal migration: reduced jobs, lower wages, overburdened schools, hospitals that are so crowded you can't get in, increased crime, and a depleted social safety net. Tolerance for illegal immigration is not compassionate; it is actually very cruel. (Applause.)

One in three women is sexually assaulted on the long journey north. Smugglers use migrant children as human pawns to exploit our laws and gain access to our country. Human traffickers and sex traffickers take advantage of the wide-open areas between our ports of entry to smuggle thousands of young girls and women into the United States and to sell them into prostitution and modern-day slavery.

Tens of thousands of innocent Americans are killed by lethal drugs that cross our border and flood into our cities, including meth, heroin, cocaine, and fentanyl.

The savage gang, MS-13, now operates in at least 20 different American states, and they almost all come through our southern border. Just yesterday, an MS-13 gang member was taken into custody for a fatal shooting on a subway platform in New York City. We are removing these gang members by the thousands. But until we secure our border, they're going to keep streaming right back in.

Year after year, countless Americans are murdered by criminal illegal aliens. I've gotten to know many wonderful Angel moms and dads, and families. No one should ever have to suffer the horrible heartache that they have had to endure.

Here tonight is Debra Bissell. Just three weeks ago, Debra's parents, Gerald and Sharon, were burglarized and shot to death in their Reno, Nevada home by an illegal alien. They were in their eighties, and are survived by 4 children, 11 grandchildren, and 20 great-grandchildren. Also here tonight are Gerald and Sharon's granddaughter Heather, and greatgranddaughter Madison.

To Debra, Heather, Madison, please stand. Few can understand your pain. Thank you. And thank you for being here. Thank you very much. (Applause.)

I will never forget, and I will fight for the memory of Gerald and Sharon that it should never happen again. Not one more American life should be lost because our nation failed to control its very dangerous border.

In the last two years, our brave ICE officers made 266,000 arrests of criminal aliens, including those charged or convicted of nearly 100,000 assaults, 30,000 sex crimes, and 4,000 killings or murders.

We are joined tonight by one of those law enforcement heroes: ICE Special Agent Elvin Hernandez. When Elvin—(applause)—thank you.

When Elvin was a boy, he and his family legally immigrated to the United States from the Dominican Republic. At the age of eight, Elvin told his dad he wanted to become a Special Agent. Today, he leads investigations into the scourge of international sex trafficking.

Elvin says that, "If I can make sure these young girls get their justice, I've [really] done my job." Thanks to his work, and that of his incredible colleagues, more than 300 women and girls have been rescued from the horror of this terrible situation, and more than 1,500 sadistic traffickers have been put behind bars. (Applause.) Thank you, Elvin.

We will always support the brave men and women of law enforcement, and I pledge to you tonight that I will never abolish our heroes from ICE. Thank you. (Applause.)

My administration has sent to Congress a commonsense proposal to end the crisis on the southern border. It includes humanitarian assistance, more law enforcement, drug detection at our ports, closing loopholes that enable child smuggling, and plans for a new physical barrier, or wall, to secure the vast areas between our ports of entry.

In the past, most of the people in this room voted for a wall, but the proper wall never got built. I will get it built. (Applause.)

This is a smart, strategic, see-through steel barrier—not just a simple concrete wall. It will be deployed in the areas identified by the border agents as having the greatest need. And these agents will tell you: Where walls go up, illegal crossings go way, way down. (Applause.)

San Diego used to have the most illegal border crossings in our country. In response, a strong security wall was put in place. This powerful barrier almost completely ended illegal crossings.

The border city of El Paso, Texas used to have extremely high rates of violent crime—one of the highest in the entire country, and considered one of our nation's most dangerous cities. Now, immediately upon its building, with a powerful barrier in place, El Paso is one of the safest cities in our country. Simply put: Walls work, and walls save lives. (Applause.)

So let's work together, compromise, and reach a deal that will truly make America safe.

As we work to defend our people's safety, we must also ensure our economic resurgence continues at a rapid pace. No one has benefitted more from our thriving economy than women, who have filled 58 percent of the newly created jobs last year. (Applause.)

You weren't supposed to do that. Thank you very much. Thank you very much.

All Americans can be proud that we have more women in the workforce than ever before. (Applause.)

Don't sit yet. You're going to like this. (Laughter.)

And exactly one century after Congress passed the constitutional amendment giving women the right to vote, we also have more women serving in Congress than at any time before. (Applause.)

Audience: USA! USA! USA!

President Trump: That's great. Really great. And congratulations. That's great.

As part of our commitment to improving opportunity for women everywhere, this Thursday we are launching the first-ever government-wide initiative focused on economic empowerment for women in developing countries.

To build on—(applause)—thank you. To build on our incredible economic success, one priority is paramount: reversing decades of calamitous trade policies. So bad.

We are now making it clear to China that, after years of targeting our industries and stealing our intellectual property, the theft of American jobs and wealth has come to an end. (Applause.) Therefore, we recently imposed tariffs on $250 billion of Chinese goods, and now our Treasury is receiving billions and billions of dollars.

But I don't blame China for taking advantage of us; I blame our leaders and representatives for allowing this travesty to happen. I have great respect for President Xi, and we are now working on a new trade deal with China. But it must include real, structural change to end unfair trade practices, reduce our chronic trade deficit, and protect American jobs. (Applause.) Thank you.

Another historic trade blunder was the catastrophe known as NAFTA. I have met the men and women of Michigan, Ohio, Pennsylvania, Indiana, New Hampshire, and many other states whose dreams were shattered by the signing of NAFTA. For years, politicians promised them they would renegotiate for a better deal, but no one ever tried, until now.

Our new U.S.-Mexico-Canada Agreement, the USMCA, will replace NAFTA and deliver for American workers like they haven't had delivered to for a long time. I hope you can pass the USMCA into law so that we can bring back our manufacturing jobs in even greater numbers, expand American agriculture, protect intellectual property, and ensure that more cars are proudly stamped with our four beautiful words: "Made in the USA." (Applause.)

Tonight, I am also asking you to pass the United States Reciprocal Trade Act, so that if another country places an unfair tariff on an American product, we can charge them the exact same tariff on the exact same product that they sell to us. (Applause.)

Both parties should be able to unite for a great rebuilding of America's crumbling infrastructure. (Applause.)

I know that Congress is eager to pass an infrastructure bill, and I am eager to work with you on legislation to deliver new and important infrastructure investment, including investments in the cutting-edge industries of the future. This is not an option. This is a necessity.

The next major priority for me, and for all of us, should be to lower the cost of healthcare and prescription drugs, and to protect patients with preexisting conditions. (Applause.)

Already, as a result of my administration's efforts, in 2018, drug prices experienced their single largest decline in 46 years. (Applause.)

But we must do more. It's unacceptable that Americans pay vastly more than people in other countries for the exact same drugs, often made in the exact same place. This is wrong, this is unfair, and together we will stop it—and we'll stop it fast. (Applause.)

I am asking Congress to pass legislation that finally takes on the problem of global freeloading and delivers fairness and price transparency for American patients, finally. (Applause.)

We should also require drug companies, insurance companies, and hospitals to disclose real prices to foster competition and bring costs way down. (Applause.)

No force in history has done more to advance the human condition than American freedom. In recent years—(applause)— in recent years, we have made remarkable progress in the fight against HIV and AIDS. Scientific breakthroughs have brought a once-distant dream within reach. My budget will ask Democrats and Republicans to make the needed commitment to eliminate the HIV epidemic in the United States within 10 years. We have made incredible strides. Incredible. (Applause.) Together, we will defeat AIDS in America and beyond. (Applause.)

Tonight, I am also asking you to join me in another fight that all Americans can get behind: the fight against childhood cancer. (Applause.)

Joining Melania in the gallery this evening is a very brave 10-year-old girl, Grace Eline. Every birthday—(applause)—hi, Grace. (Laughter.) Every birthday since she was four, Grace asked her friends to donate to St. Jude's Children's Hospital. She did not know that one day she might be a patient herself. That's what happened.

Last year, Grace was diagnosed with brain cancer. Immediately, she began radiation treatment. At the same time, she rallied her community and raised more than $40,000 for the fight against cancer. (Applause.) When Grace completed treatment last fall, her doctors and nurses cheered—they loved her; they still love her—with tears in their eyes as she hung up a poster that read: "Last day of chemo." (Applause.) Thank you very much, Grace. You are a great inspiration to everyone in this room. Thank you very much.

Many childhood cancers have not seen new therapies in decades. My budget will ask Congress for $500 million over the next 10 years to fund this critical lifesaving research.

To help support working parents, the time has come to pass School Choice for Americans' children. (Applause.) I am also proud to be the first President to include in my budget a plan for nationwide paid family leave, so that every new parent has the chance to bond with their newborn child. (Applause.)

There could be no greater contrast to the beautiful image of a mother holding her infant child than the chilling displays our nation saw in recent days. Lawmakers in New York cheered with delight upon the passage of legislation that would allow a baby to be ripped from the mother's womb moments from birth. These are living, feeling, beautiful babies who will never get the chance to share their love and their dreams with the world. And then, we had the case of the Governor of Virginia where he stated he would execute a baby after birth.

To defend the dignity of every person, I am asking Congress to pass legislation to prohibit the late-term abortion of children who can feel pain in the mother's womb. (Applause.)

Let us work together to build a culture that cherishes innocent life. (Applause.) And let us reaffirm a fundamental truth: All children—born and unborn—are made in the holy image of God.

The final part of my agenda is to protect American security. Over the last two years, we have begun to fully rebuild the United States military, with $700 billion last year and $716 billion this year.

We are also getting other nations to pay their fair share. (Applause.) Finally. Finally. For years, the United States was being treated very unfairly by friends of ours, members of NATO. But now we have secured, over the last couple of years, more than $100 billion of increase in defense spending from our NATO Allies. (Applause.) They said it couldn't be done.

As part of our military build-up, the United States is developing a state-of-the-art missile defense system.

Under my administration, we will never apologize for advancing America's interests.

For example, decades ago, the United States entered into a treaty with Russia in which we agreed to limit and reduce our missile capability. While we followed the agreement and the rules to the letter, Russia repeatedly violated its terms. It's been going on for many years. That is why I announced that the United States is officially withdrawing from the Intermediate-Range Nuclear Forces Treaty, or INF Treaty.

Perhaps—(applause)—we really have no choice. Perhaps we can negotiate a different agreement, adding China and others, or perhaps we can't—in which case, we will outspend and out-innovate all others by far. (Applause.)

As part of a bold new diplomacy, we continue our historic push for peace on the Korean Peninsula. Our hostages have come home, nuclear testing has stopped, and there has not been a missile launch in more than 15 months. If I had not been elected President of the United States, we would right now, in my opinion, be in a major war with North Korea. (Applause.)

Much work remains to be done, but my relationship with Kim Jong Un is a good one. Chairman Kim and I will meet again on February 27th and 28th in Vietnam. (Applause.)

Two weeks ago, the United States officially recognized the legitimate government of Venezuela—(applause)—and its new President, Juan Guaidó. (Applause.)

We stand with the Venezuelan people in their noble quest for freedom, and we condemn the brutality of the Maduro regime, whose socialist policies have turned that nation from being the wealthiest in South America into a state of abject poverty and despair. (Applause.)

Here in the United States, we are alarmed by the new calls to adopt socialism in our country.

Audience: Booo—

President Trump: America was founded on liberty and independence, and not government coercion, domination, and control. (Applause.) We are born free and we will stay free. (Applause.)

Audience: USA! USA! USA!

President Trump: Tonight, we renew our resolve that America will never be a socialist country. (Applause.)

Audience: USA! USA! USA!

President Trump: One of the most complex set of challenges we face, and have for many years, is in the Middle East. Our approach is based on principled realism, not discredited theories that have failed for decades to yield progress. For this reason, my administration recognized the true capital of Israel, and proudly opened the American Embassy in Jerusalem. (Applause.)

Our brave troops have now been fighting in the Middle East for almost 19 years. In Afghanistan and Iraq, nearly 7,000 American heroes have given their lives. More than 52,000 Americans have been badly wounded. We have spent more than $7 trillion in fighting wars in the Middle East.

As a candidate for President, I loudly pledged a new approach. Great nations do not fight endless wars. (Applause.)

When I took office, ISIS controlled more than 20,000 square miles in Iraq and Syria—just two years ago. Today, we have liberated virtually all of the territory from the grip of these bloodthirsty monsters.

Now, as we work with our allies to destroy the remnants of ISIS, it is time to give our brave warriors in Syria a warm welcome home.

I have also accelerated our negotiations to reach—if possible—a political settlement in Afghanistan. The opposing side is also very happy to be negotiating. Our troops have fought with unmatched valor. And thanks to their bravery, we are now able to pursue a possible political solution to this long and bloody conflict. (Applause.)

In Afghanistan, my administration is holding constructive talks with a number of Afghan groups, including the Taliban. As we make progress in these negotiations, we will be able to reduce our troop's presence and focus on counterterrorism. And we will indeed focus on counterterrorism.

We do not know whether we will achieve an agreement, but we do know that, after two decades of war, the hour has come to at least try for peace. And the other side would like to do the same thing. It's time. (Applause.)

Above all, friend and foe alike must never doubt this nation's power and will to defend our people. Eighteen years ago, violent terrorists attacked the USS Cole. And last month, American forces killed one of the leaders of that attack. (Applause.)

We are honored to be joined tonight by Tom Wibberley, whose son, Navy Seaman Craig Wibberley, was one of the 17 sailors we tragically lost. Tom, we vow to always remember the heroes of the USS Cole. (Applause.) Thank you, Tom.

My administration has acted decisively to confront the world's leading state sponsor of terror: the radical regime in Iran. It is a radical regime. They do bad, bad things.

To ensure this corrupt dictatorship never acquires nuclear weapons, I withdrew the United States from the disastrous Iran nuclear deal. (Applause.)

And last fall, we put in place the toughest sanctions ever imposed by us on a country.

We will not avert our eyes from a regime that chants "Death to America" and threatens genocide against the Jewish people. (Applause.) We must never ignore the vile poison of anti-Semitism, or those who spread its venomous creed. With one voice, we must confront this hatred anywhere and everywhere it occurs.

Just months ago, 11 Jewish-Americans were viciously murdered in an anti-Semitic attack on the Tree of Life synagogue in Pittsburgh. SWAT Officer Timothy Matson raced into the gunfire and was shot seven times chasing down the killer. And he was very successful. Timothy has just had his 12th surgery, and he is going in for many more. But he made the trip to be here with us tonight. Officer Matson, please. (Applause.) Thank you. We are forever grateful. Thank you very much.

Tonight, we are also joined by Pittsburgh survivor, Judah Samet. He arrived at the synagogue as the massacre began. But not only did Judah narrowly escape death last fall, more than seven decades ago, he narrowly survived the Nazi concentration camps. Today is Judah's 81st birthday. (Applause.)

Audience: (Sings "Happy Birthday.") (Applause.)

Mr. Samet: Thank you!

President Trump: They wouldn't do that for me, Judah. (Laughter.)

Judah says he can still remember the exact moment, nearly 75 years ago, after 10 months in a concentration camp, when he and his family were put on a train and told they were going to another camp. Suddenly, the train screeched to a very strong halt. A soldier appeared. Judah's family braced for the absolute worst. Then, his father cried out with joy, "It's the Americans! It's the Americans!" (Applause.) Thank you.

A second Holocaust survivor who is here tonight, Joshua Kaufman, was a prisoner at Dachau. He remembers watching through a hole in the wall of a cattle car as American soldiers rolled in with tanks. "To me," Joshua recalls, "the American soldiers were proof that God exists, and they came down from the sky." They came down from Heaven.

I began this evening by honoring three soldiers who fought on D-Day in the Second World War. One of them was Herman Zeitchik. But there is more to Herman's story. A year after he stormed the beaches of Normandy, Herman was one of the American soldiers who helped liberate Dachau. (Applause.) He was one of the Americans who helped rescue Joshua from that hell on Earth.

Almost 75 years later, Herman and Joshua are both together in the gallery tonight, seated side-by-side, here in the home of American freedom. Herman and Joshua, your presence this evening is very much appreciated. Thank you very much. (Applause.) Thank you.

When American soldiers set out beneath the dark skies over the English Channel in the early hours of D-Day, 1944, they were just young men of 18 and 19, hurtling on fragile landing craft toward the most momentous battle in the history of war.

They did not know if they would survive the hour. They did not know if they would grow old. But they knew that America had to prevail. Their cause was this nation and generations yet unborn.

Why did they do it? They did it for America. They did it for us.

Everything that has come since—our triumph over communism, our giant leaps of science and discovery, our unrivaled progress towards equality and justice—all of it is possible thanks to the blood and tears and courage and vision of the Americans who came before.

Think of this Capitol. Think of this very Chamber, where lawmakers before you voted to end slavery, to build the railroads and the highways, and defeat fascism, to secure civil rights, and to face down evil empires.

Here tonight, we have legislators from across this magnificent republic. You have come from the rocky shores of Maine and the volcanic peaks of Hawaii; from the snowy woods of Wisconsin and the red deserts of Arizona; from the green farms of Kentucky and the golden beaches of California. Together, we represent the most extraordinary nation in all of history.

What will we do with this moment? How will we be remembered?

I ask the men and women of this Congress: Look at the opportunities before us. Our most thrilling achievements are still ahead. Our most exciting journeys still await. Our biggest victories are still to come. We have not yet begun to dream.

We must choose whether we are defined by our differences or whether we dare to transcend them.

We must choose whether we squander our great inheritance or whether we proudly declare that we are Americans.

We do the incredible. We defy the impossible. We conquer the unknown.

This is the time to reignite the American imagination. This is the time to search for the tallest summit and set our sights on the brightest star. This is the time to rekindle the bonds of love and loyalty and memory that link us together as citizens, as neighbors, as patriots.

This is our future, our fate, and our choice to make. I am asking you to choose greatness.

No matter the trials we face, no matter the challenges to come, we must go forward together.

We must keep America first in our hearts. We must keep freedom alive in our souls. And we must always keep faith in America's destiny that one nation, under God, must be the hope and the promise, and the light and the glory, among all the nations of the world.

Thank you. God bless you. And God bless America. Thank you very much. Thank you. (Applause.)

REFERENCES

Books

1. Buchanan, Patrick J. *Right from the Beginning.* Boston: Little, Brown, 1988.

2. Buckley, William F. *Athwart History: Half a Century of Polemics, Animadversions, and Illuminations—A William F. Buckley Omnibus.* Edited by Linda Bridges and Roger Kimball. New York: Encounter Books, 2010.

3. Chua, Amy. *Political Tribes: Group Instincts and the Fate of Nations.* London: Penguin Press, 2018.

4. Churchill, Winston. *Churchill: The Power of Words—His Remarkable Life Recounted through His Writings and Speeches.* Selected, edited, and introduced by Martin Gilbert. Cambridge, MA: Da Capo Press, 2012.

5. Codevilla, Angelo. *The Ruling Class: How They Corrupted America and What We Can Do about It.* New York: Beaufort Books, 2010.

6. Gavin, William F. *Street Corner Conservative*. New Rochelle and New York City: Arlington House Publishers, 1975.

7. Hanson, Victor Davis. *The Case for Trump*. New York: Basic Books, 2019.

8. Jenkins, Roy. *Churchill: A Biography*. New York: Plume Publishing, 2001.

9. Klein, Edward. *Guilty as Sin: Uncovering New Evidence of Corruption and How the Democrats Derailed the FBI Investigation*. Washington, DC: Regnery Publishing, 2016.

10. Laskas, Jeanne Marie. *Hidden America: From Coal Miners to Cowboys, an Extraordinary Exploration of the Unseen People Who Make This Country Work*. New York: Penguin Random House, 2013.

11. Manchester, William. *The Last Lion: William Spencer Churchill*. 3 vols. (*Visions of Glory, 1874–1932; Alone, 1932–1940; Defender of the Realm, 1940–1965*). Boston: Little, Brown, 1983–2012.

12. Myer, Frank S. *What Is Conservatism?* New York: Holt, Rinehart, and Winston, 1964.

13. Roberts, Andrew. *Churchill: Walking with Destiny*. New York: Viking, 2018.

14. Sorial, George A. and Damian Bates. *The Real Deal: My Decade Fighting Battles and Winning Wars with Trump*. New York: Broadside Books, 2019.

15. Trump, Donald J., with Meredith McIver. *Trump: How to Get Rich*. New York: Random House, 2004.

Websites

1. Bugajsksi, Janusz. "Trump's Criticisms Have Reinvigorated NATO." The Hill, February 7, 2019. https://thehill.com/opinion/national-security/428920-trumps-criticisms-have-reinvigorated-nato.

2. Bunson, Matthew. "Sen. Feinstein Grills Catholic Nominee: 'The Dogma Lives Loudly within You.'" *National Catholic Register*, September 7, 2017. http://www.ncregister.com/blog/mbunson/sen.-feinstein-grills-catholic-nominee-the-dogma-lives-loudly-within-you.

3. Cesca, Bob. "Shocker: Trump and Barr Refuse to Defend Ban on Female Genital Mutilation." Salon.com, May 14, 2019. https://www.salon.com/2019/05/14/shocker-trump-and-barr-refuse-to-defend-ban-on-female-genital-mutilation/.

4. Chasmar, Jessica. "Robert Johnson, BET Founder, Praises Trump's Economy: 'I Give the President a Lot of Credit.'" *Washington Times*, July 9, 2019. https://www.washingtontimes.com/news/2019/jul/9/robert-johnson-bet-founder-praises-trumps-economy-/.

5. "Churchill's Deadly Decision: Preview." *Secrets of the Dead*, PBS, April 16, 2016. https://www.pbs.org/wnet/secrets/churchills-deadly-decision-preview-this-episode/548/.

6. Cox, Jeff. "Trump Has Set Economic Growth on Fire. Here Is How He Did It." CNBC Markets, September 7, 2018. https://www.cnbc.com/2018/09/07/how-trump-has-set-economicgrowth-on-fire.html.

7. Diamond, Max (Reed College). "Students Launch Libertarian Club at Small Oregon College and Get Harassed, Investigated, Condemned." The College Fix, June 21, 2017. https://www.thecollegefix.com/students-launch-libertarian-club-small-oregon-college-get-harassed-investigated-condemned/.

8. Drabold, Will. "Read Peter Thiel's Speech at the Republican National Convention." *Time*, July 22, 2016. https://time.com/4417679/republican-convention-peter-thiel-transcript/.

9. EMILY's List v. Federal Election Commission, Civil Action No. 05-49 (U.S. District Court for the District of Columbia, February 25, 2005). Campaignlegal.org. https://campaign-legal.org/sites/default/files/1341.pdf.

10. "Full Text: Donald Trump 2016 RNC Draft Speech Transcript." Politico, July 21, 2016. https://www.politico.com/story/2016/07/full-transcript-donald-trump-nomination-acceptance-speech-at-rnc-225974.

11. Gold, Hannah K. "Donald Trump's Life and Career: A Timeline." *Rolling Stone*, September 9, 2015. https://www.rollingstone.com/politics/politics-news/donald-trumps-life-and-career-a-timeline-50459/.

12. Goodkind, Nicole. "Democrats Accused of Anti-Catholic Bigotry by Knights of Columbus over Trump Judicial Nominee Questioning." *Newsweek,* December 24, 2018. https://www.newsweek.com/democrats-catholic-bigotry-trump-knights-columbus-1270859.

13. Green, Emma. "Bernie Sanders's Religious Test for Christians in Public Office." *The Atlantic*, June 8, 2017. https://www.theatlantic.com/politics/archive/2017/06/bernie-sanders-chris-van-hollen-russell-vought/529614/.

14. "Here's Judge Gorsuch's Full Opening Statement." NBC News, March 20, 2017. https://www.nbcnews.com/news/us-news/here-s-judge-gorsuch-s-full-opening-statement-n735961.

15. International Churchill Society. *Famous Quotes and Stories.* "No One Would Do Such Things." https://winstonchurchill.org/resources/quotes/famous-quotations-and-stories/.

16. Lederman, Josh. "Trump Administration Launches Global Effort to End Criminalization of Homosexuality." NBC News, February 19, 2019. https://www.nbcnews.com/politics/national-security/trump-administration-launches-global-effort-end-criminalization-homosexuality-n973081.

17. Marshall, William. "Donald Trump: America's Winston Churchill?" Townhall, March 28, 2019. https://townhall.com/columnists/williammarshall/2019/03/28/donald-trump-americas-winston-churchill-n2543898.

18. McIntyre, Jamie. "Here Is How Much Ground ISIS Has Lost Since Trump Took Over." *Washington Examiner*, December 23, 2017. https://www.washingtonexaminer.com/heres-how-much-ground-isis-has-lost-since-trump-took-over.

19. Piper, Greg. "Former Mizzou Professor Melissa Click Gets Contract Renewed at Gonzaga: 'She Has Excelled.'" The College Fix, September 14, 2017. https://www.thecollegefix.com/former-mizzou-professor-melissa-click-gets-contract-renewed-gonzaga-excelled/.

20. "President Donald J. Trump Stands Up for Religious Freedom in the United States." Whitehouse.gov, May 3, 2018. https://www.whitehouse.gov/briefings-statements/president-donald-j-trump-stands-religious-freedom-united-states/.

21. "Professor Makes Students Recite 'Anti-American' Pledge of Allegiance." Fox News Insider, December 8, 2014. https://insider.foxnews.com/2014/12/08/metropolitan-state-university-professor-makes-students-recite-anti-american-pledge.

22. "Queen Gifts Trump a Churchill Book on World War Two." Reuters, June 4, 2019. https://www.reuters.com/article/us-usa-trump-britain-gifts/queen-gifts-trump-a-churchill-book-on-world-war-two-idUSKCN1T516X.

23. "Read Supreme Court Nominee Brett Kavanaugh's Full Opening Statement." PBS News Hour, September 4, 2018. https://www.pbs.org/newshour/politics/read-supreme-court-nominee-brett-kavanaughs-full-opening-statement.

24. Schleifer, Theodore, and Kevin Liptak. "Trump Brings Churchill Bust Back to Oval Office." CNN, January 20, 2017. https://www.cnn.com/2017/01/20/politics/trump-churchill-oval-office/index.html.

25. Schneider, Howard. "Trump Is Right, Jobs for Black Americans Abound. Here's Why It May Not Last." Reuters, November 25, 2018. https://www.reuters.com/article/us-world-work-minority-employment-insigh/trump-is-right-jobs-for-black-americans-abound-heres-why-it-may-not-last-idUSKCN1NV0CM.

26. Stewart, Emily. "Donald Trump Rode $5 Billion in Free Media to the White House." TheStreet, November 20, 2016. https://www.thestreet.com/story/13896916/1/donald-trump-rode-5-billion-in-free-media-to-the-white-house.html.

27. "Thucydides, Pericles' Funeral Oration." University of Minnesota Human Rights Library. http://hrlibrary.umn.edu/education/thucydides.html.

28. Trump, Donald J. "President Donald J. Trump's State of the Union Address." Whitehouse.gov, February 5, 2019. https://www.whitehouse.gov/briefings-statements/president-donald-j-trumps-state-union-address-2/.

29. ———. "Remarks by President Trump at a Salute to America." Whitehouse.gov, July 5, 2019. https://www.whitehouse.gov/briefings-statements/remarks-president-trump-salute-america/.

30. ———. "Remarks by President Trump at the 2019 United States Air Force Academy Graduation Ceremony, Colorado Springs, CO." Whitehouse.gov, May 30, 2019. https://www.whitehouse.gov/briefings-statements/remarks-president-trump-2019-united-states-air-force-academy-graduation-ceremony-colorado-springs-co/.

31. Wagner, Meg, Brian Ries, James Masters, and Veronica Rocha. "President Trump in the UK." CNN, July 13, 2018. https://www.cnn.com/politics/live-news/trump-uk-visit-2018/h_8310ae4d4fd15657086af9710834186d.

32. Ward, Antonia. "ISIS's Use of Social Media Still Poses a Threat to Stability in the Middle East and Africa." The RAND Blog, December 11, 2018. https://www.rand.org/blog/2018/12/isiss-use-of-social-media-still-poses-a-threat-to-stability.html.

33. Warfare History Network. "Hitler Nearly Took Over France's Battleship Fleet. Then Winston Churchill Stepped In." *The National Interest*, August 1, 2019. https://nationalinterest.org/blog/buzz/hitler-nearly-took-over-frances-battleship-fleet-then-winston-churchill-stepped-70496.

34. United States v. Games Perez, 695 F.3d 1104 (10th Cir. 2012). FindLaw. https://caselaw.findlaw.com/us-10th-circuit/1592134.html.

35. U.S. Department of Justice letter from Noel J. Francisco, Solicitor General, to Senator Dianne Feinstein, Committee on the Judiciary, U.S. Senate, April 10, 2019, Int.nyt.com. https://int.nyt.com/data/documenthelper/766-letter-congress-female-mutilation/d448fe5dbad9f5720cd3/optimized/full.pdf.